SURVIVORS AND THE MEDIA

Ann Shearer

**BROADCASTING STANDARDS COUNCIL
RESEARCH MONOGRAPH SERIES: 2**

John Libbey
LONDON · PARIS · ROME

British Library Cataloguing in Publication Data

Shearer, Ann
 Survivors and the media. – (Broadcasting Standards Council)
 Research Monograph: no. 2
 I. Title II. Series
 384.540941

ISBN: 0 86196 332 6
ISSN: 0956 9073

Published by
John Libbey & Company Ltd, 13 Smiths Yard, Summerley Street, London
SW18 4HR, England.
Telephone: 081-947 2777: Fax 081-947 2664
John Libbey Eurotext Ltd, 6 rue Blanche, 92120 Montrouge, France.
John Libbey - C.I.C. s.r.l., via Lazzaro Spallanzani 11, 00161 Rome, Italy

© 1991 John Libbey & Company Ltd. All rights reserved.
Unauthorised duplication contravenes applicable laws.
Printed in Great Britain by Whitstable Litho Ltd, Whitstable, Kent, U.K.

SURVIVORS AND THE MEDIA

BROADCASTING STANDARDS COUNCIL

5-8 The Sanctuary
London SW1P 3JS

Tel: 071-233 0544
Fax: 071-233 0397

Contents

	Foreword – *Lord Rees Mogg*	1
1	Introduction	3
2	The Survivors	7

3	The Event
	    Survivors' experience of the media
	        Timing
	        Intrusion and harassment
	        Inaccuracy and distortion
	        Questions of detail
	        Times of trial
		13

4	The Aftermath
	    Changes in viewing behaviour
	    Fiction
		27

5	Towards Boundaries?
	    Limits of acceptability
	    The Watershed
	    Styles of television reporting
	        The Hillsborough disaster
	        The murder of a child
	        Rape
	        Road traffic accidents
	        In general
		33

	Appendix 1: The surveys	57
	Appendix 2: Viewing behaviour	61
	Appendix 3: Acceptability of television reports	63
	Appendix 4: The author and other contributors	65
	Broadcasting Standards Council publications	67
	The Broadcasting Standards Council	69

Acknowledgements

The Broadcasting Standards Council would like to acknowledge its thanks to the Victim Support schemes and self-help groups for their assistance throughout this project; British Satellite Broadcasting for helping to fund the study; the research interviewers who worked on it; and most importantly the survivors who agreed to participate.

FOREWORD

During 1989, when the Council was engaged in preparing the Code of Practice which it published in the autumn of that year, it carried out a long series of consultations with groups and individuals. A frequent topic in these discussions was the broadcasters' treatment of the series of major disasters which occurred about that time. It led the Council to include a section in its Code which set out some of the principles which the Council felt should apply in such circumstances.

Subsequently, in conversations with various organisations which provide help and give counsel to the survivors of these disasters, it seemed appropriate, as part of the Council's concern with standards to explore the issues further. In the following year therefore, it commissioned two pieces of research, whose nature is described and whose results are set out in the following pages.

The survivors interviewed are drawn from some individual tragedies such as murder and rape, as well as from well-publicized major disasters and, although the study was mainly concerned with broadcasting, some of the responses reported here arise from the conduct of the press.

The Council believes that one of its roles in maintaining and improving standards in broadcasting is to contribute to an informed debate about major issues. It was for that reason that it launched the series of Monographs, of which the present volume is the second. It is with that object in mind that I commend the book to all those who have an interest in the responsible handling by the broadcasting media of a matter which clearly is one of considerable concern to the public.

The views expressed in these Monographs will not necessarily be those held by the Council.

Lord Rees-Mogg

1 INTRODUCTION

Most people in Britain do not have to learn to survive, to live on, after being involved in a major human-made disaster, after a rape or assault, or after the sudden and violent death of a relative by murder or accident. This report is about some of those who do, for whom such tragedies have become real – and particularly about how they perceive the media's part in that process. But in a sense it is also about anyone who reads a newspaper, listens to the radio or watches television, because for all of us it is through those media that we touch, however fleetingly, that range of human experience from which most of the time we are mercifully protected.

The report is based on two studies commissioned by the Broadcasting Standards Council. The first was among a demographically representative sample of 1050 people contacted door-to-door to complete a questionnaire; it happened that one fifth of them had survived an act of violence, either as individuals or in a major, nationally-reported disaster. The second study of in-depth interviews, partly funded by British Satellite Broadcasting, was much smaller and was not designed to be representative of any national grouping, but included survivors of some of the most frequent crimes, or of a well-publicized event. Fifty-four people who had suffered the death of a (usually adult) child by murder, or had suffered rape, or sexual abuse, or assault, or who had either been involved in, or had relatives involved in, a fatal car accident or major disaster, responded to an appeal to submit to lengthy interviews. (Details of the surveys and the respondents are in Appendix 1).

To those who have experienced such tragedies, you might perhaps expect, the role of the media must be trivial by comparison with their own perceived sense of reality. After all, as one mother whose child had been murdered said:

> "This is a two-minute report, but it is a lifetime for us."

And after all again, how can even the fullest of television coverage compare with having lived through the event itself? As a survivor of one of the disasters found:

> "It didn't seem as horrific seeing it on TV as what I had been through. My experience was so horrific, the TV coverage couldn't show it."

At first glance, the large-scale survey seems to confirm that there is not much to worry about in the way the media reacts to such tragedies. A full three-quarters of its respondents, including the survivors, felt that there was nothing in the way that news was broadcast that offended them or was in 'bad taste'. That percentage rose to 83 among those under 25 years old. Yet behind those bland figures – and particularly in the experiences of the survivors in the small in-depth survey – there is a very different story, which raises important issues for both the press and broadcasting.

Some certainly found the media coverage helpful, like these survivors of disasters:

> "Extremely helpful ... they did their own investigation ... a remark made by someone who was interviewed said the rescue boats went the wrong way ... delayed rescue by 15-30 minutes."

> "They are very much on our side, but they're handicapped by red tape."

> "Just the fact that it got coverage helps. We don't want it forgotten."

Yet these relatively positive experiences were far outweighed by negative ones. The survivor of rape who said:

> "I think they should bring a law out to protect victims from reporters"

put it most strongly. But over and over again the bad experiences are reported: of learning of the tragedy not from the police, not from relatives, but cruelly from the media itself; of intrusion into and harassment of families at times of huge vulnerability; of reports that veered from the hurtfully inaccurate to the wilfully sensational. Nor did these end with the event itself: those same charges are levelled at the media when the case became once more newsworthy, when the perpetrator of the crime, for instance, came to trial. And those who felt themselves victims of such treatment also felt helpless in the face of it, as did this mother of a murdered child:

> "You can make a statement, but they'll take out of it what they want, they'll twist it ... the best thing is to say nothing, and hope something else happens that day."

And did they feel able to complain? As another mother explained:

> "No, because you can imagine the state I was in at that time. Now, I would ... I was so wrapped up in the loss of my daughter ... now I'm fuming and if there was any way I could get back at them ... but it's too late now ... ."

At the very least, for one survivor of rape:

> "They were not deliberately callous, they were just totally insensitive and couldn't care less so long as it was a good story ... just didn't think ... just appalling ignorance."

This sample was certainly small. It was certainly self-selected too, through appeals through different Victim Support schemes and self-help groups and through an appeal on the radio, and so might be supposed to have drawn those with a particular grievance that they wanted to air. But what these survivors said is not unexpected. In 1989, for instance, a resolution at the annual meeting of the National Association of Victims Support Schemes drew attention to members' perceptions that the media's abuse of privacy of victims had reached unprecedented levels. Victim Support's 1990 report on *Victims of Crime and the Media* underlines that perception. Out of 80 families of murder victims, for instance, there was only one which reported helpful and sensitive contact with the media. For 50 others, that contact had been distressing and unhelpful; their stories of invasion of privacy, harassment, publishing of details unknown to families, find echoes in the present Survey.

Is this what 'the public' wants? And if it is, should they get it? In fact, as the large-scale survey shows, it is not only victims and survivors who feel critical of media coverage. A quarter of the respondents in the large-scale survey – and especially older ones and those in higher income brackets – were offended. The picturing of the bereaved in an emotional state, the interviewing of bereaved relatives and of victims, and the showing of dead bodies were particularly distressing. (And the first troubled a higher percentage of survivors in the quantitative study than of the sample as a whole – the only time the survivors stood out from the general sample). Over a quarter of respondents felt that broadcasters should be careful about what went out before 9.00 p.m. (which is, of course, the policy adopted by the broadcasters through the use of the Watershed), and this proportion rose to a third among respondents over 55 and among women. Many people felt that certain scenes should never be transmitted, or only put out after the 9.00 p.m. Watershed.

So the concern is not restricted to people who have been victims of violence themselves. Nor is it a new one for the public. As the Broadcasting Standards Council knows from its own previous research, very many people say they are willing to condone violent acts – in particular, to protect the family, defend the country, or to prevent cruelty to animals or violent crime. But most people are sceptical that 'hard violence' can be justified in fiction, and concerns about violence extend to news coverage. People appreciate that violent images may define the importance of a news story. But only two out of ten in the Council's 1989 Annual Survey were willing to sanction close-ups of dead or wounded passengers in a train crash; there was a general feeling that the privacy of survivors and relatives and the dignity of the dead must be protected (Broadcasting Standards Council, *Annual Report 1988-89*).

Our attitudes to portrayals of violence, then, as to its reality, are deeply mixed. And that is perhaps hardly surprising. It is through such portrayals, after all, that most people first try their approach and test their reactions to the event that they profoundly hope will not happen and profoundly know must: death itself. The popularity of horror films and the like, and the way in which some people visit scenes of disasters, show that necessary fascination with violence and death in adult lives, just as devotion to traditional fairy tales does in children's ones. Our shying away from too much 'reality' in news broadcasts shows how much we fear too close a glimpse.

A 'victim', in its first dictionary definition, is a living creature offered as sacrifice to propitiate a deity. And there is something apotropaic still perhaps in our uneasy fascinations: a warding off of the evil by taking it in small, homeopathic doses. Only small ones, mind. One of the most striking findings of the large-scale survey was that significant minorities of the respondents consistently criticized television coverage of disasters ranging from the sinking of the Zeebrugge ferry to the Ethiopian famine to the Hungerford massacre, not just because it was too explicit, but because there was *too much* of it. 'Humankind', as the bird noted in T S Eliot's *Burnt Norton* 'cannot bear very much reality'.

(An insistent memory, lost until I started reading these surveys. Very green as a junior reporter, I was detailed once to hotfoot to a local canal where a child was thought to have drowned. My reaction was a panic of fantasies: was I really to see that small dead body? Worse, was I really to 'get the story', to ask the mother how it felt to her? I refused to go. The news editor read me a sharp lecture about the realities of the job, the responsibilities of the press, the continuing scandal of the unfenced canals. Thank goodness, the child was found safe and well before I had to test my fantasies against a tragic reality.)

The issues that thread their way through this report are hardly new. Where does respect for the privacy of individuals give way to a public 'right to know' – and 'need' as well? How much often horrifying detail do our jaded senses need before we can be moved, through fear and pity, to realisation of the reality of violence and its consequences? What does it take to galvanize 'the public', and thence those with power and influence, to inquire and report and try to ensure that such tragedies are minimized in future? Are the excesses of some branches of the media – and the excessive acts of others – to be curbed, and if so, how, and is there any way in which those who have suffered them can get redress and compensation? Questions like this have exercised not just individuals and watchdog bodies but the courts as well. When the Court of Appeal ruled in May 1991 that a few people who suffered psychiatric illness after watching the Hillsborough disaster unfold on television were not, although relatives of those in that crowd, entitled to compensation from the police, no fewer than 150 other Hillsborough claims and more than 60 similar actions launched in the wake of the Zeebrugge disaster were also affected (*Independent*, 4.5.91).

The Broadcasting Standards Council has made its own response to the issues in its Code of Practice. To paraphrase: to ban scenes of violence, either from 'real life' or as elements in entertainment would, it says in its Code of Practice, be to go against 'all the experience of everyday life and create for broadcasting a world constantly at odds with the real world'. Yet at the same time, broadcasting should do nothing to inflame already exaggerated fears of just how violent this society is perceived to have become. And while the often bloody consequences of violence should not be 'glossed over', neither should they be lingered on 'unwarrantably'. Only in the rarest of circumstances should broadcasting dwell on the moment of death itself. Re-broadcasts of violent scenes or flashbacks (which Victim Support has found to be particularly distressing, especially to people from Northern Ireland), should be very restricted. Accurate reporting is essential. Victims must not be exploited when in shock. Crime and criminals must not be glamorized.

Just what makes for glossing over or unwarranted dwelling, for exploitation or glorification can, of course, be endlessly debated. This report is one contribution to the debate, this time from the point of view of survivors of violence themselves. First, it introduces them and their experiences. Then it considers their reactions to the media coverage of their own tragedy, before examining the way their experience has changed their viewing habits and their own suggestions for boundaries for reporting violent crime, accidents and disasters. So it tries to go at least some way towards responding to the cry of one survivor:

> " ... *people like morbid things, they do ... it's about time TV started to show that people on our side of the fence have got feelings too and our lives are never the same again ... .*"

2 THE SURVIVORS

"At the time, it's like you're in a book or horror film, and when it's finished you'll be back to normal ... but you're not ... ."

"I'm a changed person through what has happened in my life. No-one will hurt me again."

"I think it's made me into a better person ... a stronger character ... After the court, I think I can do anything now, I can go into any situation."

The 54 survivors in the qualitative survey had been living with their tragedy from anything between a few months and a few years. How they were doing that, of course, had at least 54 different answers. At one level, they were surviving very different sorts of experience: to lose a close relative in a major, nationally-reported disaster is not at all the same as losing a close relative in an unreported traffic accident, or a child by murder. To survive an event which involved hundreds, even thousands, of others is not at all the same as to survive the most intimate personal invasion that is rape, and that experience is different from assault. At another level, each person will react to personal tragedy in their own unique way, in their own unique set of personal circumstances.

Yet at the same time, these 54 survivors had some important experiences in common. They had all suffered sudden, violent loss: of a loved life, of their own bodily integrity. They had lost too, perhaps, their innocence of death: through their experience they were forced to acknowledge its power in their own life and the lives of those they loved. Certainly they had lost their sense of controlling their personal world; taken for granted assumptions had been shattered into the experience of helplessness.

Sudden death, the experts say, throws a thicker blanket of shock over those left behind than any other kind. They have had no opportunity to prepare for their loss, no chance to finish outstanding business with the one who suddenly is not there. They have been reminded in the most powerful way of human mortality; their search for meaning, for blame, for retribution may be pressing. Sudden violent deaths can stir the worst fantasies of mutilation, destruction and killing, and leave the bereaved person feeling particularly vulnerable and threatened.[*]

Whether the individuals in this study had survived a disaster, a rape, the murder of a child, their immediate reaction could be the same.

---

[*] Beverley Raphael, *The Anatomy of Bereavement*, Hutchinson Education 1985.

> *"Complete shock – absolutely numb ... wasn't able to cope with anything."*
>
> *"(10 days later) I realized I'd been in shock. You can't think straight you know, you're letting other people do the thinking for you."*
>
> *"I didn't go out or watch TV ... We don't really know what was said, we were too numb to watch."*

Sometimes, the shock effect of a sudden death may be so overwhelming as to induce what is called Traumatic Stress Syndrome. Traumatic memories persistently preoccupy and intrude, invoking feelings of panic and powerlessness over and over again. Dreams and nightmares of the scene and memories of the moment of death keep returning. The shock of the death is so great that the individual's psychic energy is quite taken up with trying to master the feelings that threaten to overwhelm, leaving little for the processes of mourning. Sometimes, too, those who survive a major disaster may wonder why they had been so chosen and feel guilty that they should have their life when others have died. The major defence against this 'survivor guilt' is psychic numbing, and that may last for a long time.

Certainly some of the survivors in this study found the effects of their experience to have been very long-lasting. Here is how life seemed to some of those who had been involved in major disasters:

> *"People think that you've had a very bad bout of 'flu, but by now you should be over it. They don't understand."*
>
> *"It doesn't take 2 or 3 months to get over it – it is not physical anymore, it is in me. I have to live with this for the rest of my life."*
>
> *"The first year was easier because we were still numb. It's got worse."*
>
> *"Three months after it, people expect you to be normal again."*
>
> *"You say 'When was it?', it hurts because you don't remember, whereas I won't forget."*
>
> *"I was at least 2 months before getting back to work."*
>
> *"I was in deep shock for 12 months, it's getting worse, not better. The pain is with us all the time."*
>
> *"You go from extreme shock, to sorrow and anger, then back again – the emotions repeat themselves."*

Just how people do live through grief and mourning depends, say the experts, on their relationship with the person who has died, the manner of the death and their psychological and social circumstances. The attitudes of these survivors of disasters and fatal accidents (not all of whom were necessarily bereaved) give some flavour of what living on may mean to individuals:

> *"It concentrates your mind on how frail life is. I used to say I'd do this tomorrow. I'm more inclined to make the most of the day, to make the effort to make the most of what is available ... I see life in a far more positive way now."*
>
> *"One doesn't plan as much for the future, you tend to live life on a day-to-day basis. Problems seem very small ... ."*

2 THE SURVIVORS

"I look at things differently – make something of your life – it's so short."

"We are frightened now – realize how vulnerable we all are ... We have become very negative and the smacks that life deals you seem worse now – we can't seem to think positively and get on with life."

"I'm over-protective now and tend to worry all the time."

"I haven't worked since ... I tried ... but it was all so unimportant ... silly, trivial, pointless."

"After the accident I couldn't even cook a meal for the family. I had to close the business straightaway – I couldn't cope."

"We worry about our son whenever he is out ... and if he's late my husband goes out in the car combing the streets."

Individuals have their own reactions. Yet one thing that most of the survivors with whom we are concerned had in common was that private loss had become, to some degree, public property. Sometimes that could be a comfort, as it seemed to this person who felt denied the support of public concern:

"If people die in a disaster such as the Clapham Rail disaster, they get a lot of support and sympathy, but if you lose someone in a road accident in ones and twos, it isn't taken seriously. We all suffer just as much but no notice is taken."

Often though, the catapulting of private grief into the public glare, and at a time of great vulnerability, was hard. For these survivors of rape it brought, perhaps, a cruel echo of their own experience of the most intimate and literal invasion of their most personal territory.

"Exposed me terribly ... although I'd done nothing wrong, the social pressure from it being in the papers and everybody knowing about it is dreadful actually. I went into a cafe about two or three days after the rape with ... and people were talking about it at the next table, and that's pretty horrifying really."

"I think it horrified me when I realized how public it had become."

"The most distressing thing on the television was ... one of the things that happened while he was raping me. That was pretty hard, to think that they took what was a life and death situation for me and used it as a piece of news."

"It was our tragedy, not the world's. It was our tragedy."

Survivors often share another particular source of stress: the inevitable complications of the law's demands.

The law's involvement could start with the police who brought the news of the death – and that, as these mothers of murdered children found, could be a very mixed experience overall:

"(Police) were very kind ... in fact they were marvellous. There was a Chief Superintendent and another policeman. They answered all our questions and left a 'phone number we could call anytime ... ."

> " ... two police officers arrived at the scene ... the two police involved were really nice, very upset ... the WPC needed counselling later ... ."

> " ... The original officer who came was very young and did not know how to tell us. He did not know how much he could tell us. The Serious Crime Officers were absolutely marvellous ... ."

> " ... this policewoman said '—'s dead' and I just went berserk, and she said to (daughter) 'who's this?' and (she) said 'it's my mum' and the policewoman said 'Oh shit, I didn't know his mum lived here!!!' "

At times, it seemed, the demands of legal processes could overwhelm the needs of individuals, as this mother found:

> " ... we didn't have any counsellor or any WPC stay with us. They just came and took statements. One PC used to call but they took him off the case ... only the one seemed to care. The others – six in a day sometimes, in pairs, just wanted their questions answered, that's all ... ."

The way that survivors were treated by the forces of law and order is not, of course, the concern of this study. But the survivors themselves felt strongly that they wanted these aspects of their stories to be heard. For some of the survivors of rape and assault, the police were 'marvellous', 'wonderful' and 'helpful'. But for this one survivor of rape, it seemed that the police had no interest in her, betraying her confidence in their keenness to catch the rapist:

> "I was devastated in a way because I believed that my identity would be protected ... I really felt confident reporting it. The fact that they (the police) didn't believe me, it's really dreadful! ... They talked to everybody I knew. They talked to all my friends, they talked to my colleagues at work, they even went to the salaries office ... they invaded my privacy to an extent which was almost, well, was probably more traumatic than the rape. I haven't had too much difficulty in coming to terms with the rape. I have had a lot of difficulty coming to terms with the way the whole thing was handled by society."

> "The police believe rapists far more easily than they believe the victims and I'm not the only one to say that."

At a time when the sense of loss of control over their world may be one of the hardest of survivors' emotions, the demands of the law may seem simply to exacerbate the helplessness. Lack of information can make hard experiences harder.

> "The police are only interested in the boy who did it. The police have no legal obligation to inform us of anything. My PC was a nice bloke and as helpful as he could be ... Not enough contact with the police – you have to wait for the funeral, wait for the trial. One 'phone call a week from them would have made so much difference."

Most fundamentally, perhaps, people often had no control over the body of their relative. For the parents whose children had been murdered, or died in a disaster, the body ceased to be 'theirs'.

> "When — died, no-one told us that the murderer is entitled to another post-mortem ... nobody told us that, so we were sat waiting, like, 'why can't we get her buried' because she'd had one post-mortem and time was going on, and like when they die, all you can

> think about really is burying them, and we couldn't, but nobody said why ... A friend of mine went to the police station, and it was 'Oh well, you've got to wait for the second post-mortem' but nobody said about it ... We should be told more ... people should be told what goes on ... ."

> "We weren't allowed to see the body – it becomes the property of the Crown. I asked the Padre to go and pray over her body – even he couldn't ... The police regarded the body as a piece of evidence. My needs were ignored."

> "They wouldn't let me identify her ... I was a puppet in their hands ... her hair was her feature ... I just wanted to see even that. They must listen to us parents if we want to see the body ... it would have been painful, but I could have said goodbye."

> "I was told not to see my daughter's body, so I didn't and now I regret it. People shouldn't tell you what they think is best. I shall always regret not seeing her."

Feelings of helplessness, exposure and vulnerability may be triggered once more at the time of the trial. Parents of murdered children could lack information even about dates and times of the trial; its speed, and the verdict too, could leave some people feeling that less than justice had been done.

> "I didn't realize the court case would upset me so much ... I was a nervous wreck ... you feel as though you are on trial. It's awful, you can't protect that person ... they're no longer here to answer for themselves ... ."

Most of the survivors of rape and sexual abuse found the process of the trial a worse experience, they said, than the attack itself; they would think twice about reporting another, should it happen. Having survived the trial, they felt stronger – but it was strength bought at a high cost.

> "When it happens, it's only you that it's happening to, nobody else is there, nobody else is watching, nobody else is listening, and that is it. And then in the courtroom, everybody knows, everybody's listening, everybody's judging, and you're trying to think 'Did it happen this way, or did it happen that way?' And it's really hard to try and remember."

> "When I think now ... I think, 'Would I rather be raped again or go to court', then I'd rather be raped again than go to court."

> "The actual rape itself has left me with less scars than the way it was handled – that's terrible, a terrible indictment of society that a rape can be easier to recover from than the inquiry afterwards, the trial and the rest of it."

And finally, how does this society evaluate the suffering sustained by survivors? One woman pointed out how her life – and that of others – had been damaged by the man who assaulted her. Yet he was now out of prison and receiving state help and had apparently suffered less than she had. Another had found little compensation for suffering:

> "I did try to apply to the Compensation Board because of my lack of income. It will take over a year. I'm disgusted with the system – you need the money then, not a hundred years later."

What survivors do underline is just how complex and difficult an area the media finds itself in when it sets out to report on such tragedies.

The representatives of the media may find themselves, it seems from this study, sometimes bearing news that people least want to hear, details that horrify. They may be seeking news and details that people least want to give. Either way, the people with whom they are interacting are likely to be numbed with shock, liable to say things that later they may regret. How can such messengers hope to escape being shot?

Media involvement may also key into some of the survivors' most difficult experiences. At a time when one of their most fearful emotions may be the sense that they have lost control of their world, the media may, by wrenching private grief into the public realm, simply underline and exacerbate that sense of helplessness. Or, perhaps and sometimes, not. For some people, telling their story and telling it as publicly as possible, may be helpful. As one survivor put it:

> "There are some who want to shout and others intensely private ... it's down to the families."

For at least one survivor whose relative had been killed in a fatal car accident, the very fact that the story *was not* told was additionally painful:

> "No-one was interested in our story ... (she) was just another road accident."

For others again, intense media interest which then, and inevitably, fades to none at all, may bring its own particular hurt, acting as a trigger to that intense suspicion of 'false' nurturing which is one of the characteristics of 'survivor guilt'.

So how right can the media hope to get it? There may be another dimension to consider too. 'With his whole emotional being it seems,' says the psychoanalyst John Bowlby, 'a bereaved person is fighting fate, trying desperately to turn back the wheel of time and to recapture the happier days that have been suddenly taken from him. So far from facing reality and trying to come to terms with it, a bereaved person is locked in a struggle with the past.' So it is, he says, both unnecessary and unhelpful for friends or therapists to cast themselves in the role of 'representative of reality' to the bereaved person – unnecessary because he or she is, in some part of themselves, well aware that the world has changed, and unhelpful because by disregarding the world as another part still sees it, they alienate themselves from them.[*]

Media folk, of course, are neither friends nor therapists to survivors. Their role is precisely, however, to be that unnecessary and unhelpful 'representative of reality' – however distorted their version of reality may seem to the survivor or be in fact. Just how that uneasy relationship may be played out is what the next section is about.

---

[*] John Bowlby, *The Making and Breaking of Affectional Bonds*, Tavistock Publications, 1979

3 THE EVENT

Survivors' experiences of the media

> "I'm a great believer in the freedom of the press, but it's not freedom, it's just a licence, and there's a difference, and I don't think it's done with any respect by some parts of the media. Not to have any respect for or care about the feelings of the people involved ... ."

> "It does hurt but the thing is it was news, and you have got to make people aware of this."

> "Some are offended by whatever is reported."

Between them, most of the 54 survivors interviewed for the qualitative survey had experienced – and endured – the attentions of the full range of the media, from local and national newspapers and radio to both the BBC and independent television companies.

That media reporting of their case was both necessary and helpful, many survivors had no doubt. As we have seen, for some, the opportunity the media offered for their story to be heard could itself be healing. In very particular cases, like the immediate broadcasting of news of a major disaster, the radio especially could perform a vital function in alerting relatives to contact police and give essential descriptions earlier than they might otherwise have done.

> "Very informative – told the facts and didn't offend anyone."

> "They gave all the facts as soon as they knew them."

> "Lots of updates when bodies were found ... I wanted all the information I could get."

> "Very sympathetic – gave helpline numbers."

The media could play a valuable part, too, in keeping alive the issues raised by disasters, chivvying the authorities through their own investigations: 'they are very much on our side', as one survivor perceived it. More immediately, radio and television could play their part in helping police to find criminals – as these survivors of assault and rape discovered:

> "(After the radio interview) so many people came forward and gave the police descriptions and accounts of what happened. A taxi driver came forward and said he had picked up — and gave the police a description."

> "They did get one or two calls you know. It was on the television the next night, and at least one or two motorists 'phoned in the police station and they went in for interviews. They'd actually seen him when he went along the road."

Yet if the media's speed of action and discovering and reporting of details had these positive aspects, they also had some extremely negative ones. These survivors told story after story of the hurt they suffered through the *timing* of media attention, through *intrusion* into their privacy and *harassment*, through *inaccuracy*, *distortion* and *distasteful detail* in what was reported.

Given the circumstances in which these survivors and the media met, it is perhaps hard to think of any timing that could have been 'right'. And as is well known, what seems distortion to the person most intimately involved with an event may look like objectivity to the outsider, showing one more time that perspective is in the heart and eye of the beholder. And, again, the contact of these survivors with the media was very often at a time when they were numbed with shock. Those involved in disasters, particularly, might have little or no awareness of how the initial coverage of their case was done.

> "We were shielded by good friends ... we knew it had been on but no-one told us anything in detail."

> "People around me kept me away from a radio."

> "You have to remember people might see it, but if they're personally involved, it's a blur – you don't perhaps realize you're numb."

Yet the anger and hurt of these survivors was consistent. It ran across the different groups. And it continued over time, triggered when interest in the cases was revived by a trial or an inquiry – often the more distressing because the survivors' initial protective numbness and shock had by then thawed.

This report is primarily about survivors' experiences of *broadcasting*. But to leave out their views on the press would be to distort the picture. For every group, newspapers were clearly the worst offenders, and certain sorts of newspapers at that, as one survivor of rape discovered:

> "I'm aware now there is a very different standard of reporting in the 'respectable' papers ... they don't report sex crimes the way the tabloids do ... (Newspaper) is intolerable."

Although no section of the press was immune from criticism, for some people, like this woman whose child had been murdered, the local press came out well:

> "The locals were a lot better ... they behaved a lot differently to the national papers. They were concerned that we lived in the area ... I don't know whether they get more time. The nationals go on hearsay and a quick 'phone call ... ."

Yet others, like these survivors of assault, were most critical of local newspapers – perhaps because these were the ones that carried most reports.

> "My age was wrong, my name was wrong ... ."

> "They made statements that were totally incorrect. We insisted on an amendment to the statements which they printed in a distorted form."

> "They only reflected his side of it, they didn't find out the truth about what happened. It was just completely lies what was in the paper."
>
> "They made it seem like she (daughter) was telling lies because no one else was there."
>
> "The nice, ordinary friend who was stabbed was portrayed to be a real romeo! They were distorted enough to give people the wrong impression of what happened and what he was like."

And for one woman who had been raped, and who had her case reported in both local and national press, it was one particular local newspaper that had so hounded her family and friends that it had drawn the threat of a police prosecution.

> "I'll never ever trust a reporter again. He printed things I was supposed to have told him and I hadn't -I never once had an interview. Even when the police gave a press conference, I was sat in that room so I knew what the police were saying – but it was still reported wrong ... I'll never forgive him (the reporter)."

Negative experiences of the press were certainly not universal:

> "The girl who came and interviewed me for the article was good ... she printed just about everything I told her, she didn't put anything in, like they say the papers do."

But this woman who had been raped reflected a pretty general view:

> "The newspaper is just out for the story ... the news is out for the story but it's more ... I think the TV's better, especially national, not just your local. It's much better, and it's much more factual and although it's after a story, it's quite concerned ... for the victim."

Broadcasters cannot, however, afford to be complacent about their own approach. As we will see, many of the criticisms that were directed particularly against the press could be, and were, applied to radio and television on occasion too. Before exploring these criticisms in detail though, it seems worth looking at a more general question: Is one news medium more intrinsically suited to dealing with these particularly sensitive cases than any other?

For some of these survivors, radio had particular advantages. As one, who had been involved in a disaster, said:

> "It isn't vivid – no pictures."

Yet for one woman who had been assaulted – and whose preference would have been for no reporting of her case at all – the radio was more threatening than newspapers because, like television, it was already in the home.

> "Really the radio is worse than the newspaper in that you can avoid reading the papers, but the radio is already in your house."

Suddenly to hear a broadcast about your case with no warning whatever could be, as we shall see, extremely distressing. Yet for one survivor of rape, the problems had not been with broadcasting, which she *had* generally been able to avoid, but with the press. She had:

> "... kept the paper cuttings because they were real, they were solid, physical. I could

hold them, whereas what you hear can get distorted with time. So I'd say that the papers were the things that hurt the most because they seemed more real."

The power of the visual impact of television – and the way that its shocking images remained alive – drew comment particularly from those who had been involved in disasters.

"The pictures were too vivid – mum watched it not knowing if her son or daughter had been killed ... it should have been censored."

"All I see is that boat on its side and I think that my daughter was in there."

"They always focused on the boat – which was rather distressing."

Yet for another survivor, it was not television which had fixed the most painful image, but a newspaper:

"They don't always think about how the parents feel if they can see their daughter smashed across the front of (Newspaper) ... I think that's quite horrifying ... they (TV) didn't show pictures that were too long, they were quick flashes ... quick over one person being crushed, next person being carried away."

In short, there seems to be no 'best medium' for the reporting of painful news. But what did emerge strongly from the survivors' views is that there are plenty of ways in which the media can make tragedies more difficult to bear.

Timing

"My daughter heard first ... we didn't hear first ... a local paper 'phoned her up and said ... 'Do you have a brother' __? She said 'Yes'. He said 'Well he's been stabbed, is that right?' That was the first we heard ... ."

*"This happened at around (evening). My mum, who's got heart trouble ... we couldn't get hold of her that night and we got the police to go round there, I think around half-nine in the morning, and it had been on the half-seven news, the eight ... If she'd have heard that, on the radio, it could have killed her. They had **NO right** to put it on the radio until the relatives had been informed ... ."*

One of the most common complaints from those whose child had been murdered was that they had either actually first heard of the death from the media or that relatives ran that risk. There did seem to be an extraordinary and potentially agonizing lack of co-ordination and organisation between police and media on this. And not surprisingly, it aroused very strong feelings.

Newspapers and the radio seemed to cause the most distress on this critical point.

"I can't really remember a lot of what happened that day, all I know is that I was taken to the police station to make a statement, and the reporters were all knocking on neighbours' doors ... I think it was either the (Newspapers) ... reporters were over at the shop as well ... but I didn't actually see anybody. The (Newspaper) was also at her —'s in —and she'd only just that minute been told — was dead when they knocked at the door ... so like another 5 minutes and the reporters would have told her ... ."

"There was one (Newspaper) ... came for a photo ... kept 'phoning up, and when we got

3 THE EVENT

back from — they were hanging around ... and they'd been to our neighbours, who hadn't actually known, and it was a shock ... ."

"It was on all morning, but we hadn't had the radio on, so we hadn't heard it ... as far as we knew, — was still at his mate's flat."

"(BBC Radio), we didn't hear it. I've got an 86 year old father! Sometimes they keep the name back ... this time they didn't. We weren't allowed to tell people before they heard it ... ."

"I just wish they hadn't said anything till later, to give time for us to tell people ... it wasn't held back whatsoever ... ."

The power of television to reach across the country could bring its own hazards:

"A bit on the BBC news on that day ... but it never got referred to again ... it's amazing how the family even in — got to hear of it ... ."

So the way television gathers its news and the way it presents it could be something of a blessing.

"By that time, we had managed to contact everyone ... ."

"I saw it the night I came home from the mortuary after seeing her, and it was on then, but it just stated that a man had been arrested, and that was it ... ."

For these survivors, the role of the police brought its own questions.

"(Senior Police Officer said) ... you're lucky it wasn't out sooner ... ."

" ... the police should have told us how — died. After arguing most of the night ... they gave in to my brother and said all we can tell you is —. That's the police's fault ... we told them how offended we were and they apologized ... Highly unethical to hear it that way, but that was not the media's fault, it's the police who give them the details ... ."

" ... why can't they tell the Press – 'OK, we know you know, but can you hold on to it, because we haven't got hold of his mother to tell her' ... ."

"If they (the police) don't play ball with them (the media), they give the police a hard time, but if they give them the information they want as soon as they can have it ... then they stop harassing the police ... . There are moles in the system who, as soon as 999 calls come through, they alert the Press ... ."

In a major disaster, the situation is of course very different. What has happened is often reported live, or immediately after the event, before all the victims have been identified or their relatives told. Sometimes the first that relatives heard of the accident was on the news.

"Terrible shock ... I ran out of the house and tried to look for her like a mad thing."

"All that night we 'phoned the hospitals through the numbers on the screen."

"At 6 o'clock it said on the News that seven people were missing and one body had been found. The number of dead and missing went on going up until it reached 50."

"I had to keep going to the police station – we kept hearing on the radio – another one was found."

> "My mum was very distressed, watching the TV as the disaster unfolded."
>
> "After that it was on and each time you saw them lifting people up ... (my daughter) was saying 'That looks like her'."

For these people, however, the fact that it was through the media that they first heard of the tragedy did not seem to cause major distress. This was in sharp contrast to those involved in the murder cases. Media reports, as we have seen, could actually be helpful to them. And in the stress of waiting for information about their relative, the source of their information seemed of minor concern.

For other survivors again, the fact that their cases should be reported immediately after the event seemed entirely proper.

> "In principle, I don't think they should not report rape – I think they should report it, but in a constructive way."

So for these – and indeed pretty well all of the survivors – the issue is not whether or not the tragedy should be reported straight after it has happened, but *how* it is reported.

Intrusion and harassment

> "They went up to the school, they laid wait at the end of the school drive. They were approaching the children, primary schoolchildren, to ask them ... They wouldn't care, they'd approach one of the girls and say 'One of your classmates has been killed this morning, how do you feel about it?' Awful, heartless, wicked, WICKED!"
>
> "It was continued harassment by reporters ... they appeared everywhere, even putting on white coats at the hospital to crash in and hassle people."
>
> "The Press were calling out that some of the missing had been found (all lies) to try and get them to come out and give them a story and some photos."
>
> "At 8.30 the following morning the local press were knocking on our door. They called through the letter box that if we didn't give them an interview they would print what they had even if it wasn't right ... It was very upsetting."

These memories from people involved in a murder and major disasters are just the start of the indictment of the 'newsgathering' methods of certain newspapers. The recollections of some of those involved in cases of murder have the quality of nightmare.

> "If they had approached us in a reasonable way, we would have talked to them, but they approached other people, for instance — and offered £x for a photo, and they approached — saying we had given permission to get a photo."
>
> "Bombarded ... I was protected ... a freelance spoke to my husband and said 'I'm going to write it anyway, better to give one'. It was emotional blackmail ... ."
>
> "With papers like that, they're always digging up the dirt, and another thing, they were offering money, the cheque book was out ... yes, that was the morning she'd just died ... she'd only been dead a couple of hours ... ."

"They just kept ringing and ringing ... and they were here in (the street) with their cameras ... knocked on all the neighbours' doors ... were pushy, not pleasant."

"They bullied their way in here ... they asked me for a photo of — on their wedding day ... They don't care what they say, they've got no feelings ... ."

But these respondents found that the radio was not always blameless either.

"They hassle you a bit when you are feeling upset. They asked me silly questions about how I felt, and I was feeling dreadful ... ."

"They pestered me with 'phone calls ... desperately wanted me personally to go on air."

"He was hounding us all the next day ... ."

And television did not escape censure either from those involved in murders.

"They were lying in wait ... they came forward with their TV cameras – like a fool, I didn't just walk on ... I bolted into a doorway ... I was stuck, there was nowhere to go without being filmed ... ."

Most hurtful of all, perhaps, could be media coverage of the funeral.

Sometimes the press was there.

"A funeral is a private affair; we weren't besieged, but I could see them behind a tree with a camera, a still camera ... ."

"The local paper came up to my husband at the cemetery and said 'Could we take a photo of you and your wife by the flowers?' (Husband): 'I was stood there arguing with the bloke ...' ."

Sometimes television joined in.

"I had a 'phone call on the morning of his funeral and this man said, 'I'm a friend of —'s, can you tell me what time the funeral is, from the house and down at the Crem.' I said 'what's your name', and he said 'I might as well tell you, I'm a reporter' ... I thought that was a very sneaky way of finding out ... ."

"On the morning of the funeral, they were right across the road, pointing a camera at the window. I turned round to (ITV) and said 'why don't you jump in on top of the bloody coffin, then you'd get a close-up shot' ... I did get the impression that if they could actually get inside the coffin with a camera, they bloody would ... ."

At least the radio waited for an invitation.

"The local radio 'phoned up and asked if they could go to the church. They did ask ... ."

Two things are particularly worth emphasising in this dismal tale of intrusion and harassment. The first is that it seems that of all the respondents, it was those involved in murder who suffered its worst excesses. The second is how powerless, at that most vulnerable time, they felt in the face of this. The police, presumably, could anticipate the sort of media attention that would fasten on to these cases. In one instance, they helpfully arranged that the relatives gave a statement to a news agency which meant that they were bothered only by local papers. In another, they arranged for the endless stream of telephone calls to be blocked. But more often, their assistance seemed to be restricted to a warning not to give interviews. And about that, some people were dubious.

> "I gave my views ... I think you should, otherwise they make it up ... ."

> "I thought, if you don't talk to them, they'll go elsewhere ... they'll knock on other doors, and they're not going to get the truth, are they ... ."

What to do? If you do not talk to them, they may just go ahead anyway (as two survivors of assault also found). Neither of them wanted publicity. Both got it.

> "I felt in no fit state to discuss it further and I felt they were intruding ... I asked for no publicity to be given, and yet it was emblazoned in banner headlines all over the front page of the paper."

> "They should have respected my wishes if I wanted anything reported ... It could have caused me to crash. It just came on the radio when I was driving home. It was such a surprise. It made me feel I could not face people again. It was a long time before I went to town."

Inaccuracy and distortion

> "They didn't do anything wrong. It was very factual. I think they didn't think it was newsworthy enough to go any further, which I'm very grateful for ... ."

> "It was just a small announcement. They didn't get it right at all. They said he had been shot ... there's a lot of difference in being shot and being battered to death ... ."

> "It was totally unrealistic reporting – untruths that had badly affected the issues ... they got everything wrong."

> "Basically it wasn't actually interested in what happened."

Many of the survivors commented on inaccuracies in reports about their cases. Sometimes, perhaps, it was hardly possible that it should be otherwise: to be accurate about the final scale and details of a disaster as it is unfolding just cannot be done. Yet even here there was criticism of the radio coverage:

> "Initial reports gave the dead and missing total much more optimistic than it turned out to be."

> "The slightest piece of information is reported and can do a great deal of harm ... dreadful for the parents."

At other times, though, the media cannot plead immediacy in mitigation. What emerged clearly from these survivors' accounts is how hurtful inaccuracies in reporting can be, even – and perhaps especially – small ones. For people whose world has just gone out of control, whose integrity has been shattered, seeing or hearing that world portrayed in a way that just is not true can only, perhaps, increase the sense of helplessness, confusion and loss.

As one woman said of the radio report of the murder:

> "I would have made sure that all the facts were right ... her age was right, the area we

> *lived in was right, niggly things ... we* don't *live in — that annoyed me. And the ages of my children were all wrong ... ."*

When does inaccuracy become distortion? Again, people could feel helpless when it seemed that their own words had been twisted – like these survivors of, first, a murder and then, a disaster:

> *"It made me sound aggressive, which I'm not. The fact that he got x years didn't do anything for me ... I wasn't pleased, but the way it came over was I felt that — should have gone to prison, and that wasn't me ... ."*

> *"They're so cunning ... we did say some of the things reported ... but they turn it around."*

Sometimes, according to these people in like situations, the press did not even wait for an interview:

> *"The way they wrote it, I had given a statement to the Press. But if you read it very carefully, it obviously wasn't. The next morning, one of the CID said ... 'Did you speak to the Press?' and I said 'No' and she said 'They've reported it making it sound as though you did' ... It's unfair, it's not right ... they're very clever the way they worded it ... They distorted it with their use of language ... you couldn't say they'd told a lie ... ."*

> *"Whatever I said they didn't print – they printed their own and put my name to it."*

For one victim of assault, reporting seemed damagingly one-sided:

> *"It made me sound like the guilty party – like I deserved the attack and what I got ... (the reporter) didn't bother to find out the whole story before he wrote the piece. This bloke wrote a totally incorrect piece."*

Once more it was the press which was most heavily criticized. But for these survivors of murder, television and radio could also distort things:

> *"Bits and pieces are shown out of context through no fault of the reporter ... The people who control the news programme decide what should be shown to make the best programme ... ."*

> *"In one (radio) reporter's words, 'We only report the juicy bits'. It wasn't a balanced report ... I would have liked them to speak to us – I would have asked them to report both sides of the story as the local paper did ... ."*

> *"The (radio) interviews were taped, but cut up and broadcast out of context and made me sound very bitter. I gave several interviews, but I wasn't happy with the editing. I would only take part in a live one now ... ."*

> *"(The radio) should just report the case ... the facts. They try to get an argument going between the two people, I think ... ."*

When does distortion become untruth?

> *"We've got no gripes about the police ... the next day the paper printed that we weren't happy with the way the police had dealt with the situation, which was totally unfair, because we were quite happy (with them) ... ."*

"One (paper) reported a sexual attack, but this was just made up ... ."

"(The popular press) said supporters were robbing the dead. Told lies."

"(The radio) just mentioned the (injuries) and not all the rest as if it didn't matter. They said that we were lovers and I'd broken it off which was not true."

And finally, the way that people involved in these tragedies are described, again mostly by the press, can be extremely hurtful. What may look like useful shorthand may appear a cruel dismissal of the dead person to those who are mourning. What may appear a 'good angle' from one perspective can be the most wounding sensationalism and stereotyping from the other.

"I rang them when I read the report just after her murder ... I know it didn't have any bearing on the crime ... but it upset me when I read that she was just a (occupation) ... ."

"It sounded to me like as if they're making — sound like a knife-wielding, drunken lout, a lager lout ... it was unjust."

"One headline said, 'Death of the beautiful people', and went on to add that they were models and photographers, and implied that they were all wealthy and glamorous ... it was completely untrue ... It prejudiced public opinion against them."

And once the labels are applied, it seems, they can stick.

"(ITV) still put on that it was a fight between lager louts, a drunken brawl ... which was totally wrong, it was proven in court ... ."

Questions of detail

"They didn't name — but they gave all the details ... Strange to hear the name of —'s killer, and all the details ... really the police should have told us that, instead of hearing it on TV. We were so hungry for information ... desperate ... and we were getting it from the media rather than the police ... ."

"I'm not sure if it's allowed. They should have consideration for who's been told. I don't think it's necessary to give out details of how someone died. The youngest child found out how his sister died from the radio ... The majority of the family found out how she died over the radio, before we had time to tell them."

"Someone went to my son and said, 'That was your mother that was raped wasn't it?' — knew from the papers ... anybody who knew me identified me from the information they put out and initially I was too traumatized, I think, to worry about it, but after a while I began to realize that nearly everybody I knew knew that I had been raped. Everybody!"

One way to minimize inaccurate and distorted reporting is to pay scrupulous attention to detail. But too much detail, as the above quotations show, can add hugely to survivors' pain and difficulties. The questions raised touch on the apparent lack of co-ordination between police and media on release of information, referred to earlier. They touch, of course, on the way that media attention inevitably brings private distress into the public arena. Yet there is nothing inevitable about broadcasting or printing details that identify the victims of, say, rape or assault.

3 THE EVENT

One survivor of rape, however, was identifiable by the way the press described the family and where they lived. To underline the point:

"The television cameras made sure they shot the house as they went by!"

– and the shot was shown.

This sort of identification can lead to an abrupt curtailing of choice for the survivor in whom she tells of her ordeal, as this woman discovered when the name of the road in which she lived was broadcast on both radio and television:

"Unfortunately I lived in a road which ... only had a few houses in – if they knew they might not have done it, but ... (resulted in) people ringing up and saying 'What's happened?' 'Is it true?'"

Identification can also increase fear, as this survivor of assault (who had *not* been identified) pointed out:

"I think it's good that people's names don't get put in. You don't want people knowing it was you it happened to ... someone might do it again to you."

Identification and detail can make it hard to resume ordinary life, as another survivor of assault discovered:

"It was reported a lot in the newspapers, so people at work read it all and I found it embarrassing."

And there are some details which, for these survivors of disasters at least, should simply not be shown.

"A cameraman ran past me and filmed a boy who was dead – I swore at him."

"The cameraman ... should say 'It's a person who is crying' and should move his camera from that person ... ."

Times of trial

"Once it got to the trial 6 months later, I had it all being brought up again ... and the same photos being shown. It was like reliving the whole thing again. They could have kept a lower profile for the family's sake. At that second stage, 6 months later ... when we were trying to get ourselves together we could have done without the whole thing again."

"Why should people know? It's bad enough appearing in court without everybody knowing about it."

"I was devastated by the fact that it was in the paper and I didn't know anything about it. I didn't know about the trial."

For survivors of disasters, such renewed media interest as there had been in their case was on the whole quite acceptable. (Not all relevant legal procedures for all the survivors were complete at the time of interview, so the second wave of attention had not fully broken.) But for survivors of murder and rape, the old issues of inaccuracy, distortion of fact and too much attention to detail could be painfully renewed at the time of a trial.

Once more, it was the press which drew most comment from those involved in murder cases. Their attentions ranged between too much and hurtfully little.

> "The reporter was very kind, very honest in his reporting. The only thing we didn't like was after the verdict, they wanted a photograph of us, and we refused, but the photographer took one anyway, which was printed in the paper ... ."

> "Gory details printed ... a big play was made of mutilations ... blazoned across a placard. I had no idea it was going to be printed ... purely to make people buy the paper. No reason for that to be printed ... ."

> "Heavily reported on two occasions ... because it took 6 months before the trial came up ... it was all re-reported. (Newspaper) quoted that they interviewed me ... when they went down for manslaughter ... they said they interviewed me personally. I hadn't even spoken to them on the 'phone ... I think that was terrible, that was an out and out lie ... shouldn't be allowed ... ."

> "People said it didn't fit. I said of course it didn't ... it was a load of nonsense. People who know us know it was a load of nonsense, but a load of people who know of us still think — and that is so harsh, so unfair on her memory. It matters a lot to me ... ."

> "(Newspaper) asked for a photo and then lost it ... ."

> "— Magazine. It was never published. They caught me when I was on valium ... didn't know what to say ... and these photographs I desperately want back and can't get them back ... they're priceless ... ."

But if it was the press that people most wanted to speak about, radio also came in for criticism.

> "They didn't bother saying anything of what —'s witnesses said. We were getting 'phone calls asking why these things weren't said in court (they were) ... ."

> "All the gory details were dragged up again ... it wasn't necessary to hear all that."

> "They 'phoned up as soon as they heard the sentence ... asked me whether I would be on the radio there and then, and give my views ... Then the police 'phoned ... to tell us the result, but in fact they were a bit late. We heard what happened over the radio, about the sentence, and I just went into tears ... ."

Television was also sharply criticized.

> "They got everything wrong because they had no-one there reporting. Goodness knows how they got their information ... but it was all reported wrong ... ."

> "Showed —'s photo, it was a shock to see —'s photo, large enough to fill the TV screen. It would have been better not shown at all ... ."

> " ... it was certainly on (ITV) with a picture of one of these houses ... One doesn't know whether it was in fact your house – it may have been your neighbour's, but what difference does it make (to the media)? And what interest is it? Up comes a shot ... is it interesting? It's another something that they've taken from you. It's an intrusion of

3 THE EVENT

> *one's privacy. Someone has died – does it matter what house they lived in, or their relatives still live in? I'm not interested, if someone has ... been murdered, what sort of house they lived in, or where they worked. You're not serving any useful public function ... ."*

Most shocking of all was the experience of seeing film dating back to the murder itself, suddenly and without any warning.

> *"That really upset me and I felt ill, I felt sick ... in fact that put me back a long way. It was as if it was happening (again) ... Now, I'd take them to court. I'm quite good at being strong, but at that time we were devastated as a family – we still are, but you learn to cope with it. They kept that (film) specially for then (trial)."*

> *" ... the most horrific thing they did ... 6 months later when they got sentenced ... That night we were sitting in the front room and on the TV came up a video film of the re-enactment, and I sat there, and I had to look at — and we never knew they had been there. They had no right to show that at all. That could have put me over, that could have sent me insane. The only film that was taken was by the police, and if they got hold of it that way something's wrong ... but it wasn't a good copy ... one would assume someone was hiding somewhere ... it wasn't professional ... ."*

For the women who had been raped, the most painful aspect of reporting of their trial was the detail that was given. This could, once more, lead to identification. One woman who had moved house and job after the rape felt that the press had 'blown her cover'.

> *"(I was) identified not by name but by detail in the press and so I complained about that ... giving out information that was very likely to identify me. They gave out the location where I lived, everything, all that had been said in court was put in the paper and that was a very traumatic part of it ... my occupation, what I did, where I worked."*

More than this, though, detailed reporting could make public aspects of their story that these survivors had not themselves told anyone.

> *"When they printed all that stuff in the paper – because I hadn't told (relative) everything you see – and I thought, oh no, they're going to think I'm so bad and I was so worried ... people at work, I did care, but I wasn't going to explain it, but to (him), I thought, I want to justify myself to you ... I showed him the paper (and said) 'you've got to promise me that you're still going to be my friend after you've read it'. I was so scared about what they would think ... (he) was really upset because it really drummed into him that it actually happened to me."*

> *"I guess that whoever is responsible doesn't think: if that was my wife or my daughter, would I like ... I don't know how people can write like that, or use the media like that, if they have families of their own."*

Only one of the three survivors of rape or sexual abuse whose case had been publicly reported felt satisfied with the way it had been done. The general feeling was that there should not be extensive coverage at the time of trial or appeal. But against this, one survivor whose case had *not* been reported felt that this left unfinished business.

It was:

> "*As though it had never happened – that's how I felt it was ... there should have been something. I could have seen it saying 'it's all over now'.*"

4 THE AFTERMATH

Changes in viewing behaviour

> "If there's something on about the justice system, I'll watch it more now than I did then ... I wouldn't have been interested before ... ."

> "I always make sure that I see the news programmes first now rather than anything else."

> "I don't watch the news ... it's too awful – murders and war – no good news ... it's all depressing."

For all the survivors in the qualitative study, the effects of their tragedy were long-lasting. Their lives had been changed by it. Often their grief was continuing – exacerbated perhaps by a continuing legal involvement that might mean that they could not for months bury their dead, or that questions of compensation remained outstanding. Painful memories could be reawakened if their case came to trial – often made the more painful by the way that this was reported in the press, television and radio.

Against this background, this section focuses on how, if at all, 38 of these survivors, who responded to a semi-structured questionnaire, felt that their experiences had changed their viewing behaviour. All of them had one television in their home; most had two and a video cassette recorder as well, and most claimed to watch television for an average of three and a half to four hours a day.

The interviews took place anything between a few months and a few years after the tragedy. The sample was too small to establish whether the passage of time had any effect on the way they watched television. But what is generally clear is that they did *not*, overall, avoid potentially painful factual programmes. Instead, they found themselves more interested in these than they had been before their tragedy.

One indication of the way that these respondents saw the world – if a pretty theoretical and general one – comes from a series of statements that they were asked to rank on a five-point scale (from 'agree strongly' to 'disagree strongly'). Overall, there was not much difference in their responses according to the type of experience they had been through. Here are the statements, with the scoring in brackets (sample of 38):

Most people *agreed strongly* that –

People should be kept informed about things even if they cannot do anything about them (23/38).

People sometimes need to be shocked to make them aware of the severity of events (23/38).

Most *disagreed strongly* that –

Sometimes it is better if people are only told part of the truth (22/38).

Most *agreed* that –

I sometimes find that a television programme makes me think in a different way about an issue (32/38).

People should be allowed to express their views freely on television and radio (28/38).

I rely on television to keep me informed of what's going on (23/38).

People should be allowed to express themselves freely on any subject (23/38).

Most *disagreed* that –

There is so much violence on television nowadays that nothing affects me any more (22/38).

What did these theoretical positions mean in practice? No fewer than 22 out of the 38 said that the type of programmes they watched *had* changed since their experience. These were the sorts of programmes that most of them would specifically choose to watch:

Current affairs/documentaries	28/38
National/international news	26/38
Regional/local news	23/38
Comedy programmes	23/38
Soap operas	20/38

Some people reckoned that they were now more selective in their viewing:

"*I read the reviews before I watch to make sure of the content of these programmes.*"

"*Choosing rather than just sitting there and watching whatever comes on for the sake of it.*"

For some people, the choice was away from programmes which might be distressing:

"*We don't like to watch anything that is disturbing now ... News items are the most disturbing.*"

"*I can't watch ... tragic cases.*"

"*I can't watch anything violent.*"

> "I won't watch any disaster programmes, it brings it all back."

One survivor of rape very specifically avoided related programmes and news items 'like the one on the girl sexually assaulted in hospital'. Another pointed out how difficult it was to watch certain programmes with other people:

> "They know what's happened to you, and then something comes on the TV, you feel this awkwardness."

For another again, the effect of her experience was very widespread on both her viewing and her listening:

> "On the radio, I don't listen to 'downmarket popular shows' because they're often very sexist. I'm now very sensitized to this."

> "There's a lot of things I would have done before. I'd say I was a very conventional viewer before (but now) I don't like popular shows on TV with brainless dolly birds. I'm terribly sensitized to anything that portrays a woman as a sex object – as stupid and not knowing her own mind and dim. I don't like programmes that have those kind of 'hostess' roles in ... I'm very sensitive to anything that shows women in a victim role because I think that's exploited a lot so I won't watch films or television programmes where women get beaten up."

Some of those who avoided news and current affairs looked to television to cheer them:

> "We like comedy shows because we need to laugh now. Anything light-hearted that we can laugh at is good."

> "Just like films and things like that to cheer me up."

More generally, though, people had turned towards news and documentary programmes. Often, they found themselves particularly attracted to those which related to their own experiences.

> "I listen to more of a documentary than I did before ... I suppose I take more interest in the news things."

> "I like watching Crimewatch and discussion programmes – more so now."

> "Morbid curiosity about murders and mysteries – true ones. I just take more interest in murders and suspicious deaths and accidents now."

> "I watch all programmes now on murder cases and what prison sentences they get ... more interested in how other people get off lightly ... ."

> "I watch more programmes about road safety."

> "It doesn't even bother me if they've got cases of sexual abuse because my heart goes out to them. If it's a true-to-life story like when they were doing that Childline thing with Esther Rantzen, my heart was going out to some of the stories that they were saying about children going through that. It makes me think I'd like to help them because I've been through it and I know what it's like to go through court and I know what it's like to have been through sexual assault."

> "I'm careful about what I watch ... I guess I watch obsessively anything which is to do with rape or with victims or with the media ... I wouldn't choose to watch it because I enjoy it but I like to know what's going on.. I haven't yet recovered enough to be active about it, but the time will come when I will be ... I wouldn't choose to listen to something that was gratuitously sexist but I would watch something if I wanted to find out how bad it was because that was information for me ... (particularly just after the rape) it was really important to find out what was going on in the world. I thought I'd been really ignorant before – it's no good being an ostrich. (Now) I'd probably get pretty upset about it, but I would watch it because I'd want to know what was happening."

Finally, a specific: while 20 of the 38 said that they would want to see *Crimewatch UK* (a television series appealing for help from the public to solve real crimes, with reconstructions of some crimes) irrespective of their own experiences, a further seven said that they would want to watch it *because* of these.

Fiction

> "I think if I'm going to see someone strangled I won't (watch)."

> "I don't watch anything with murder in it – it sickens me now."

> "I avoid anything with violence in ... gratuitous violence especially. There's so many with violence ... I avoid them, I don't like emotional violence – anything that's sex, purely to titillate."

> "Can't watch murders or things like that, especially if it's a woman."

> "I don't watch horror films any more ... films where people get stabbed for the sake of it. Violence is blunting the edge of people ... ."

> "I have a sense of reality in fiction and if it was to deal with something like that (sexual abuse) and I thought it was wrong, I'd still think to myself 'well it was only a programme'. I'd just say to my husband 'that's not right' but it wouldn't bother me."

> "I look at television, and I think it's fiction ... it's only a story ... it's not real to life, it's fantasy."

These quotations, from survivors of murder and (the last two) sexual abuse, show the range of reactions to fiction which might touch on real and painful memories. All the respondents were shown a list of 11 television shows, including *Crimewatch UK*, cops and robbers shows, either indigenous or imported, or the more robust soap operas. Only Dennis Potter's *Blackeyes* (a television drama series) had not been seen by most (see Appendix 2 for the full list).

People's experiences did not seem to have much effect on whether they would watch these programmes or not. Six of the 38 claimed that they would avoid *London's Burning*, about the London fire brigade, because of their experiences. People were very partial to *The Bill* (a drama series about the police in London), but although 21 *wanted* to see it, only one of those said that was because of their experiences.

Across the list of eleven television programmes, there were 28 votes for avoidance 'due to experiences' and eight for viewing for the same reason. By contrast, there were 80 nominations for 'avoid anyway' compared with 138 for 'want to see anyway'.

The respondents were put through much the same sort of exercise on a list of 15 films, only three of which a majority had actually seen, which may have accounted for their general indifference to most. But eight did say that they would avoid *The Towering Inferno* (that favourite holiday viewing standby) because of their experiences, and seven that they would avoid *Psycho III* for the same reason. Most would avoid *Psycho III* and *Friday 13th* irrespective of their own experience (see Appendix 2 for list of films).

Overall, there were 34 votes for avoidance 'due to experiences' and six for viewing for the same reason. Nominations for 'avoid anyway' ran to 116, compared with 'want to see anyway' at 100. Left to their own devices most of these survivors would avoid horror films (25/38) and enjoy 'comedy' (27/38), 'crime/detective/thrillers' (26/38) and 'biographies' (21/38).

Four of the six rape and sexual abuse survivors had in fact particularly chosen to watch *The Accused*, a film about a rape which did not figure on the interviewers' list, one of them on the recommendation of her counsellor as preparation for her court case.

One was upset by it:

> "(It made me feel) pretty sick. The rape scenes were a real turn on. I felt they were aimed at men ... but they didn't portray it for the victim. You very rarely saw the victim's threatened position ... you saw a group of men getting very excited about a faceless woman ... so the rape scene ... was disgusting ... it's a terrifying, frightening, violent experience."

The other three were not unduly distressed. One was surprised by this:

> "I felt like I should be upset by it, but I wasn't ... what happened to her was completely different to what happened to me so I'm not trying to compare myself with her."

Overall, it seems that this small group of survivors, far from fleeing the world's harsher realities after their own experiences, became on the whole more willing to explore violence and distress in their own society and the wider world. (Other research, commissioned by the Council and undertaken by the University of Stirling,[*] which examines the attitudes of women who have been subjected to domestic violence would support this). They became, if anything, more selective in their viewing than they used to be. But their choice of fictional entertainment at any rate was dictated far less by their own real life experiences than by what they enjoyed anyway and independently of those.

None of this is to say that these survivors did not have some clear ideas about the limits of acceptability in television portrayal of the kind of events in which they themselves were so painfully involved. They did, and the final section explores their views and those of the larger quantitative sample.

---
[*] To be published in the autumn of 1991

5 TOWARDS BOUNDARIES?

"It's very important that people should see what's going on in the world – we should never shut doors on problems. If there is any problem, I'm sure someone out there is willing to help."

"It's wrong. It shouldn't be like that. Humans are so callous – even me ... we watch ... to see your loved ones dead must be dreadful. Take it back and edit it ... we don't feel other people's pain, only our own."

"Any report is going to keep the wound open, but they wouldn't be hurt any more than they already are."

The survivors were not, as we have seen, against the reporting of painful news. The interviews yield only one absolute rejection of a topic as unsuited to any news coverage at all. One of the victims of assault felt that rape should not be reported.

"Both my wife and I find this to be a repulsive topic. It's a fact of life, I agree, but we don't want to have it in our home."

But this opinion stood out sharply from those of the other survivors. Are they in fact a particularly resilient group? Well over half of those asked, as we have seen, disagreed strongly with the statement that 'Sometimes it's better if people are only told part of the truth' (22/38). About the same proportion agreed that 'People should be allowed to express themselves freely on any subject' (23/38).

Can we compare these responses from the qualitative study with fairly similar questions asked of the large general sample? Among them, just under a quarter (23 per cent) felt that 'The truth should be told even if it is upsetting'. And only 15 per cent agreed that 'Freedom of speech was important even though this might hurt other people's feelings'.

This is how the large sample finally ranked these and other questions in order of importance:

– Over a quarter (28%) said broadcasters should be careful about what is shown on the news before 9.00pm. (That proportion rose to a third among those aged over 55 and women.)

– About the same number (27%) thought broadcasters should be sensitive to victims and not transmit upsetting material. (Again, a third of women felt this.)

– Rather fewer (23%) thought the truth should be told even if it is upsetting.

This, however, was the most important statement for 35 per cent of men, and the second most important statement for respondents from Ulster.

– Only 15 per cent felt that freedom of speech was important even though it might hurt viewers' feelings, although in subsequent questioning, this statement was given a relatively high priority by other respondents. Nonetheless, sensitivity towards victims remained the second choice.

So are the survivors with whom we are concerned, at a theoretical level at least, more robust in their attitudes to painful subjects than the population as a whole? It would not perhaps be surprising if they were. As several pointed out, nothing subsequently seen on television can compare with the reality of what they had been through. And they have been into what – for most people – remains the stuff of nightmares.

That journey, as we have seen, had left many of the survivors (though not all) particularly sensitive to the world's realities. They were more inclined, after their experience, to watch news and documentaries than they had been before it, especially if these touched on tragedies comparable to their own. Here again a tentative comparison with the views of the large sample may be possible. Only just over half these respondents (53%) thought that an important story should be followed closely on the news; 41 per cent thought it should not, because it would become *'too boring'*.

The large sample was also asked for its views of actual coverage of major disasters. On the whole, there was not much criticism of this, with the often large majority finding it 'well-handled'. Where people (sometimes a fairly large minority) did not feel this, their main criticisms were not just that the coverage had been too explicit, but that there had been *too much* of it.

Table 1. Attitudes to broadcast coverage of events

	Well handled (%)	Poorly handled (%)	No view (%)
Zeebrugge Ferry	79	10	11
Lockerbie Air Crash	78	8	13
Ethiopian Famine	72	14	13
Armenian Earthquake	70	6	24
Clapham Train Crash	68	6	23
Hillsborough Stadium	66	22	10
Marchioness River Boat	66	10	22
Enniskellen Bomb	64	†9	24
Hungerford Massacre	61	15	21
Mob murder of two soldiers in Ulster	‡55	22	21

† With the strongest negatives views coming from respondents in Ulster
‡ 68% in Ulster

Limits of acceptability

The 38 survivors from the qualitative study who took part in the semi-structured interview and the respondents to the large-scale survey were all asked how acceptable they found ten hypothetical television news items (see Appendix 3 for list). It is important to note, perhaps, that while we do not know the circumstances in which the large sample considered these items, we do know that the survivors considered them *after* they had told their own, and often very painful, story to the interviewer. The more striking then, perhaps, that for *both* samples it generally seemed that the nearer the items came to the harsh individual reality of raw tragedy, the less they were acceptable.

The least acceptable items to the survivors (in the qualitative study) – and vehemently condemned by them – were these:

- The scene of a major incident, showing dead or seriously injured people who are recognisable.

- Pictures of people who have been bereaved and in a very emotional state.

- Close-up shots of blood-streaked pavements where victims fell.

The most acceptable items to this group were:

- The scene of a major incident after bodies have been removed.

- Pictures of victims being visited in hospital by members of the Government or Royal Family.

The other five items brought much more divergence of view. But, on balance, these were *acceptable*:

- Interviews in hospital with people who have been the victims of violent crime. (Interestingly, however, a majority of victims of assault rejected this item as unacceptable.)

- The scene of a major incident taken from a distance so that the dead or injured are not recognisable.

- Interviews with people in hospital suffering from a terminal illness.

And by a narrow margin, these items were *not acceptable*:

- The funeral of someone who had been the victim of a terrorist attack.

- Interviews with bereaved relatives after the death of a member of their family.

(This last is particularly interesting in that it actually ranked fifth in acceptability among people who were likely to have endured it – those who had been involved in a murder.)

Respondents to the large survey were also asked their views on the acceptability of all but one of these items. What is striking is how much agreement there was between the two samples about the most acceptable and least acceptable items.

The *least acceptable* items for broadcasting for the large sample were:

Pictures of people who have been bereaved and are in a very emotional state

	% acceptability
Completely	6 ⎫ 19
Fairly	13 ⎭
Not very	24
Not at all	55

Those in the sample who had themselves been victims felt even more strongly: 60 per cent thought such items were 'not at all' acceptable. Interestingly, this is one of only two instances when the views of the victims in the sample (see Appendix 1 for sample details) stand out from those of the large sample as a whole.

The scene of a major incident showing dead or seriously injured people who are recognisable

	% acceptability
Completely	9 ⎫ 22
Fairly	13 ⎭
Not very	23
Not at all	55

The **most acceptable** items were:

Scene of a major incident after the bodies have been removed

	% acceptability
Completely	55 ⎫ 87
Fairly	32 ⎭
Not very	8
Not at all	3

For both the survivor sample and the large one, then, the most acceptable item was one in which no human being who had any intimate involvement with the tragedy was to be seen.

Scene of a major incident from a distance so that bodies are not recognisable

	% acceptability
Completely	39 ⎫ 76
Fairly	37 ⎭
Not very	13
Not at all	10

5 TOWARDS BOUNDARIES?

Men and those living in London and Ulster were particularly likely to find this item acceptable. Overall, this response is the second instance where the views of the large sample are seriously out of harmony with those of the survivors, who were much less in favour of this item. Hard, perhaps, for 'non-survivors' to empathize with the horror of such scenes.

Pictures of victims being visited in hospital by members of the Government or Royal Family

	% acceptability
Completely	40 ⎫ 74
Fairly	34 ⎭
Not very	9
Not at all	15

The following items were **acceptable** to the large sample:

Funeral of a victim of a terrorist attack

	% acceptability
Completely	33 ⎫ 66
Fairly	33 ⎭
Not very	17
Not at all	47

This was one of the items which, by a narrow margin, was not generally acceptable to the survivors in the qualitative study. In the large sample, women found it less acceptable than men. But respondents from Ulster were particularly positive about it: 85 per cent of them found it acceptable viewing. (By comparison, the funeral of a victim of a natural disaster was even more acceptable to the large sample: 70 per cent found it completely or fairly acceptable (34%, 36%) and only 13 per cent found it not at all acceptable.)

Interviews in hospital with people who have been the victim of violent crime

	% acceptability
Completely	24 ⎫ 63
Fairly	39 ⎭
Not very	16
Not at all	17

Interestingly, in the large sample, those who were perhaps more likely to have had firsthand experience of acts of violence were *more*, not less, accepting of associated broadcasting and 45 per cent of men aged under 45 found this item completely acceptable. (By contrast, the large sample generally found interviews in hospital much more acceptable if they were with victims of natural disasters. Over three-quarters found these either completely or fairly acceptable (30%, 40%), and only 9 per cent not at all acceptable. Again, younger men were more likely to find this item completely acceptable.)

Interviews with people with a terminal illness

	% acceptability
Completely	22 ⎫ 54
Fairly	32 ⎭
Not very	19
Not at all	23

This item was far more likely to be acceptable to younger men than to the sample as a whole: 77 per cent of them found it so. By contrast, over a third of those over 55 felt it was not at all acceptable (35%). Interestingly, the division of views in the large sample, and the very small overall majority in favour of such broadcasts, echo the feelings of the survivor sample; although overall they found such items acceptable, there was more division of opinion on this topic than on the others.

The large sample also found one more item **unacceptable**:

Interviews with bereaved relatives after a death of a member of their family

	% acceptability
Completely	8 ⎫ 29
Fairly	21 ⎭
Not very	23
Not at all	44

This item was not acceptable to the survivor sample as a whole. But interestingly, respondents in the large sample were much more likely to find this item acceptable if they came from Ulster (44%). Compare this with the view of those who had been involved in a murder in the survivor sample: they ranked this item fifth in acceptability. Are those who are more likely to have firsthand experience of such items more stalwart in their acceptance of them than other people?

The Watershed

Both the group of 38 survivors and the respondents to the large sample were asked on which side of the 9.00 p.m. Watershed they felt certain items should be broadcast. The two samples cannot be directly compared because they were responding to different items. But the responses give a flavour of their views.

The *survivors* were asked to consider how much coverage should be given to six different items before and after the Watershed.

5 TOWARDS BOUNDARIES?

- Civil disturbances like Brixton, Toxteth.
- Destruction caused by terrorist bombs.
- Scenes from major football incidents, such as Hillsborough.
- Major fires, such as that at King's Cross.
- Scenes from major transport disasters, such as aeroplane or train crashes.
- Crowd disorder around sports grounds.

None of the survivors would have banned coverage of any of these items altogether, although five would *not* have shown destruction caused by terrorist bombs, scenes from major football incidents or crowd disorder around sports grounds *at all* before 9.00 p.m. On the whole, the survivors wanted early coverage of all the items restricted to 'brief facts' although some opted for 'selected pictures with commentary' in reports on civil disturbance, major football incidents, major fires and crowd disorder.

After the 9.00 p.m. Watershed, most survivors settled for 'selected pictures with commentary' for all items. But no fewer than 17 of the 38 wanted 'full coverage' of crowd disorder around sports grounds, and some wanted full coverage of civil disturbances like those at Toxteth and Brixton as well. Overall, in fact, it was on coverage of these 'public disorder' items that opinion among the survivors was most divided. (While three people who had been involved in murders, for instance, would have banned any coverage of crowd disorder around sports grounds from early broadcasts, two others would have given this *full* coverage even at this time.) Does the element of willed disturbance in these occasions of public disorder mean that people perceive a greater public 'need to know'?

Table 2. Acceptability of televising situations

	Should not be shown before 9.00 p.m. (% agreeing)
Scene of a major incident showing recognisable dead or injured	54
Pictures of bereaved in very emotional state	39
Interviews with bereaved relatives	33
Dramatic reconstruction of natural disaster	29
Interviews in hospital with victims of violent crime	27
Scene of major incident from distance so dead and injured are not recognisable	27
Interview in hospital with people with terminal illness	26
Funeral of victim of terrorist attack	20
Interviews in hospital with victims of natural disaster	20
Funeral of victim of natural disaster	18
Scene of major incident after bodies have been removed	17
Visits to victims in hospital from Government/Royal Family	12

Respondents to the large survey were asked to rank not these incidents for transmission time, but those which they had already considered for acceptability, detailed above. This means that some of these respondents would effectively be saying: 'I do not think it should go out at all, but if you must broadcast it, then it should not go out before 9.00 p.m.' Not surprisingly, the overall view of what should *not* be shown before the Watershed echoes that on acceptability, as suggested by the survivors (Table 2).

Finally, both the survivors and the large sample were asked how acceptable they found dramatic *reconstructions* – of last sightings of murder victims or missing persons (the survivors) and of violent crimes and natural disasters (the large sample).

Most of the survivors felt that these should be shown in the early evening (28/38) but there was a division of view as to whether this should be through 'selected pictures with commentary' (13), 'full coverage' (12) or 'brief facts' (5). When it came to the later evening, though, all agreed that these reconstructions should be shown and 26 of the 38 felt that there should be 'full coverage'.

Respondents to the large survey also generally felt that reconstructions (of violent crimes) were acceptable, 59 per cent 'completely' so, another 29 per cent 'fairly' and only 5 per cent 'not at all'. People who had themselves been victims were even more emphatic, with 66 per cent finding such reconstructions 'completely' acceptable. By comparison, only 64 per cent felt that dramatic reconstructions of natural disasters were either completely or fairly acceptable, while 18 per cent thought that they were not acceptable at all, and no fewer than 29 per cent that they should only be broadcast after 9.00 p.m.

Are people judging reconstructions of this sort by their potential 'usefulness'? As we will see in the survivors' responses to different television reporting styles, this is one of the most important criteria by which news coverage of different tragedies is assessed.

Styles of television reporting

Can there be such a thing as balanced and constructive reporting of what are essentially unbalanced and destructive acts? In a search for some answers, the survivors discussed three different ways of reporting four different situations: the murder of children, rape, major traffic accidents and the Hillsborough stadium disaster. All the respondents looked at each situation, not just the one most relevant to their own case. Their discussions – which were entirely about television reporting – began with them being shown large cards with the three reporting 'scenarios' outlined in writing on them. There were no pictures – other than the ones in the respondents' imaginations. Of the four situations only Hillsborough was 'real'. For this reason, discussions around it are perhaps the most revealing. Two of the survivors had actually been there. Most other people had seen the television coverage. This disaster is also the only one on which the views of the survivors and the large sample can be compared. So we start with it.

The Hillsborough disaster: three scenarios

Scenario A — Film and voice-over of events as they happened, with detailed shots of victims.

Scenario B — Reports after the event, with pictures of the ground and interviews with survivors.

Scenario C — A factual report of what happened, how many died, and what is being done to prevent another. Pictures only of the stadium by air.

The first 'scenario' was live, unedited reportage – the way, in fact, that the disaster broke into countless homes as it was happening.

To one of those who had been there, this was:

"Totally unsuitable (Interviewer: Did you switch it off?) ... No, I didn't. I wanted to see it – it was only half as traumatic as being there."

The other survivors who had themselves been involved in major disasters or fatal traffic accidents echoed the view that live coverage was simply not on.

"It disgusted me ... it shouldn't have any coverage at all."

"I think (it) was totally and utterly out of order."

"Totally unsuitable."

"Disgusting ... I know of people who saw their children suffocating on TV."

"This is a horrendous way ... no clearance for this."

"Disgraceful."

Yet only three of the eleven respondents in this group who had seen the live coverage had switched it off.

"We just cried our eyes out."

"Appalling ... I was too stunned to switch it off. I just sat there, horrified. People who watched it are still suffering after effects."

"I don't remember it clearly, but I doubt if I switched it off. It's real ... you can't hide away from reality."

"It's human nature to want to see it live."

Suggestions as to what should have happened ranged from turning off the cameras altogether, to prefacing coverage with warnings that would alert relatives, to editing the most distressing scenes.

"Shouldn't have shown people dying and fighting for life."

The respondents were concerned both for relatives and for those for whom memories of comparable situations might be painfully evoked.

"That must really hurt families ... to be crying out for help and you can't help them – I think that's very hurtful."

"Relatives would have been horrified and deeply shocked. A lot of relatives have suffered incredible psychological trauma because they watched the live coverage on TV."

"(Other survivors) would be totally traumatized – they couldn't watch it without going through it all again."

"They would relive their own experience and it would set them back emotionally."

The second 'scenario' for Hillsborough gave less detail, with edited pictures and interviews with survivors. This was more acceptable to this group, although many still had doubts.

"Yes definitely – I think you get a first hand view of what was going on."

"Yes, to see if I could find out what had caused the situation."

"No, it shouldn't ... the reports don't take the victims' feeling into it."

"No ... no need to dwell on how the survivors feel. They are obviously distressed and showing the ground where it happened only upsets everyone."

"I don't necessarily think people need to see that ... maybe it's a little revelling in other people's unhappiness."

Opinions were mixed on whether interviews should be held with survivors, notably between the two people who had actually been at Hillsborough.

"They put into words what I had gone through ... it made sense and it began sinking in."

"The survivors should be left alone. I feel reports are for those who are not involved in the disaster ... not for Hillsborough victims."

Among other respondents in this group, the balance of opinion was in favour of interviewing survivors.

"Interviewing people who are so distressed can only upset everyone watching, unless they like watching other people's misery."

"If you lost someone there it wouldn't help hearing how awful it was from a survivor."

"If the survivor feels that they need to be interviewed and tell their story, then that's down to them, and I feel that probably they'd get a lot of benefit from it."

"Interviews with survivors gives relatives relief."

"It's news ... people want to be made aware of what's happened and a detailed account given by a survivor – you can't do better than that."

And although half the respondents thought that this report would not be any easier for relatives to cope with than Scenario A, others were more matter of fact about it.

"They would have been stressed but if you've been in a disaster you're in such a shocked state it doesn't sink in."

"Be a bit more stressed ... but that's life ... at least they're alive."

"I know I would have to watch because I would want some answers."

5 TOWARDS BOUNDARIES?

The last 'scenario' these respondents who had been survivors of disasters and fatal traffic accidents considered was simply a factual report – how many died, what was being done to prevent other such tragedies – accompanied by aerial pictures of the stadium. Most people found this acceptable because it gave the facts and would cause least distress to survivors of this or other disasters.

"It's got to be told – it's news and alerts people to the dangers of what can happen."

"That's much better ... They're doing something about it ... No gory details."

"I'd be interested to see what was being done to prevent it happening again. The average person could cope with it because it's news and it's detached."

Overall, of the 16 people in this group, 9 found Scenario C the most acceptable and 10 found A the least acceptable – including the two respondents who had actually been involved with Hillsborough. But others were not so sure.

"(C is) too detached and lacks impact. People soon forget, however horrific the accident was, if reporting is too detached."

"(C) would only hold your interest for a few moments but certainly wouldn't have any impact."

"I don't think (C) is going to do any good. It just becomes another news item."

"(Scenario A) does hit home what happens at a disaster. We all think it won't happen to us – we must try and make it come home to make all things safer."

"Because it is a horrific thing for people to view it has the maximum impact on the public ... and will spur people to look for public inquiries to ensure such a tragedy could never happen again."

What did the other survivors in the study (who were *not* survivors of disasters or fatal tarffic accidents) feel about the Hillsborough coverage? Again, many had seen it on television and had been profoundly shocked. And again, many had not turned off.

"I think that's appalling to report that particular disaster in that way ... yes I saw it, but I didn't switch off because we knew two people who had gone to the match ... ."

"Devastating ... I watched it. I hadn't got anyone of my own there but it was so devastating, it was compelling, but I felt sick watching it ... ."

"It was so horrible, seeing it and not being able to do anything about it."

"What I objected to was people suffocating or nearly suffocating in front of the camera for entertainment or for news – who needs that? It's not acceptable to me ... I can understand that it is a fascinating horror as well ... it was tragic to have to watch a tragedy unfolding and be helpless to do anything about it ... there's not many people who would have chosen to stand there doing nothing, just watching people die."

"It was horrifying, terrible – I judge the television and newspapers more with carelessness and insensitivity than with deliberate callousness ... I think they don't think! They thought more about a good story and a drama than they did about people sitting at home, I think. That's terrible! Who would voluntarily want to watch somebody they loved killed in front of them? Or even know that they were somewhere in the crowd?

43

> ... I don't think it should have been shown actually ... (or) the repeats that kept coming on and on ... they were terrible! Dreadful! What good did they do, what did they achieve that couldn't have been done by a verbal report?"

Scenario B was generally thought far more acceptable – and indeed necessary.

> "You have to know what's happening, and how it happened, to maybe avoid it happening again in the future."

> "I watched it. It was news and by then I wanted to know what had happened, and what had caused it. Wanted to know what the survivors thought."

> "I was interested in some of the survivors, some had seen death and been so near to death, and they were able to tell their story, that they were survivors."

But respondents emphasized too the need to be sensitive to relatives of those involved – for whom, they felt, Scenario A would have been nothing but horrific and devastating.

> "The pictures of the ground, talking to people outside the ground, that's OK, but not interviews with people giving graphic details of people who died in the ground ... you're going to be distressing relatives ... ."

> " ... not showing the damage to the barriers and the clothing that was left ... By not showing things like people's belongings and bloodstains on the steps – it's unnecessary."

> "However it's reported, it is bound to upset some relatives and survivors, but everyone will want an inquiry into why it happened."

Scenario C was certainly acceptable. But not a few people thought it inadequate to the magnitude of the disaster.

> " ... too impersonal. It's not an individual event ... there's football matches all over the place ... not enough impact ... Wouldn't upset (relatives) as much ... (but) what is major to them is being treated in a trivial way."

> " ... it's too early to say what is being done ... they don't know what caused it. There's nothing wrong with it, but it's no value to anyone ... I don't think it's a very clever way to report it ... it doesn't do anything ... ."

> "It doesn't tell you anything. What good are pictures of the ground from the air? It doesn't really make you think about the dangers and what could happen to people."

A few people felt that, for all its horror and the distress it would bring to relatives, such a disaster demanded the coverage given in Scenario A.

> "I'd want to see it because it's a National Disaster, and sometimes we have to look at things, else they won't get changes. It must have an impact on people to get things changed."

But overall, this group reacted as did the survivors of Hillsborough itself, other major disasters and fatal traffic accidents. They opted for Scenario C as the most suitable – because it gave the facts, concentrated on prevention of any future disaster of like sort and lacked the vivid detail which was so distressing for relatives and others. And they strongly rejected the sort of live coverage offered under Scenario A.

" ... they shouldn't be allowed to show it until the relatives had been informed ... ."

Overall then, the whole sample of survivors felt that live coverage of the Hillsborough tragedy had been unacceptable for themselves and, they imagined, for relatives and those who had been involved in comparable disasters and risked having their wounds reopened. Yet at the same time, people felt it important that such a tragedy should be given enough detailed coverage to bring home the magnitude of what had happened and to galvanize action to try to prevent a recurrence. Many people felt that the witness of survivors themselves was an important element in this.

From this evidence, then, there seems to be no 'right' way to report a disaster of such dimensions – and perhaps that is not surprising. The search for a generally acceptable way of reporting is complicated by the findings of the large-scale survey. Here, fully 66 per cent (and a fifth of the total sample were survivors themselves) found that the Hillsborough tragedy had been 'well handled' on television. Yet at the same time, 22 per cent found it 'poorly handled'. And in a sample which seemed generally pretty satisfied with television coverage, there was a high level of dissatisfaction, equalled only by that felt for the coverage of the mob murder of two soldiers in Ulster. The main criticism in both cases was that the coverage was too explicit (with women feeling this most strongly about Hillsborough, and those aged under 45 emphasising it in the Ulster case). Importantly, those who had themselves been victims of individual violence or nationally-reported situations, were most likely to say there should have been a warning that bodies were going to be shown.

Do reactions to other sorts of tragedy add to a picture of acceptable reporting? Survivors in the small sample also discussed different ways in which television might cover the murder of a child, a rape and a motorway pile-up. The three 'scenarios' discussed for each (hypothetical) situation were not directly comparable. But, as with the Hillsborough ones, they moved always from the most detailed report (reconstructions of the murder or rape, and live coverage of the traffic accident) to the least embellished factual statement, with an attempt at compromise in the middle.

All the respondents discussed not just the 'case' most analogous to their own but the other two as well. In fact, overall – and perhaps significantly – there turned out to be little discrepancy of view between those who had suffered one sort of tragedy or another. The main tension for all of them was the one that we have already seen around the reporting of the Hillsborough disaster. How to achieve enough impact to honour the enormity of the event and need for action without causing more distress than necessary to those most involved and others whose painful memories of their own tragedy might be revived?

The murder of a child – three scenarios

Scenario A — Report of the case including visual reconstruction of last sighting with actors, interviews with relatives, search parties and description of how the body was found.

Scenario B   Pictures of the child's home, where the body was found, the mortuary, with the story of events as a voice-over.

Scenario C   Factual description of events, with a map of the area to show where it happened.

On the whole those whose own child had been murdered approved of the first scenario, with two important provisos – if it were going to be of help in catching the criminal and if the parents had been consulted and wanted such a report to appear.

"I would have allowed that ... if it was going to help."

"I would watch it because you can relate to the parents and know what hell they are going through ... ."

" ... if it's going to help catch the murderer ... it has to be done. That is using the television then and it's a good thing ... ."

"The relatives probably wouldn't watch it because they would know when it was being shown, but they might need to watch it. Everyone reacts differently ... ."

"The relatives would know it was going to be on, so would choose whether to watch or not ... would want to see if it was accurate ... Other relatives of victims would feel sick and angry – like me."

Even with the provisos, there was a further anxiety: that the 'description of how the body was found' would be too detailed and thus distressing, as well as potentially damaging to the hunt for the killer.

"They should not give a description of how the body was found. It gives cranks a chance to come and say they did it because they know what happened."

" ... how the body is found is superfluous – 'naked body with a cord around its neck' ... but the location couldn't be too bad."

There are, however, details and details, and these people whose own child had been murdered reacted far more strongly against Scenario B – which in fact is less 'immediate' than the first one. Their vehement feelings of disgust and horror focused particularly on the fact that the mortuary was shown, though the inclusion of the house was also very distressing.

"I think that's terrible ... I mean why a picture of the mortuary? That's horrendous ... that really upsets me ... the thought that my daughter went there. I don't think anyone needs to see that ... I think that's terrible. I mean what will that achieve except hurt to so many people ... ."

"The parents of these children don't want to think ... where an autopsy is carried out ... I think of it as a place where another abomination took place."

"Unnecessary to stand at the victim's home, because that can give sick people ... they might send a letter to the family, or a 'phone call ... some sick people who do things like that ... ."

" ... you shouldn't go to the child's home because it does invite unwanted press interest ... ."

> " ... the child's home is private and the parents have got to remember it for the rest of their lives. I can't go by the house where — lived now."

> "That's happened to me. I mean.. they do go to the mortuary, but imagine what that does to my husband, having been with her all that time, and having to go back hours later to identify her at the mortuary. I mean, to see anything like that on TV would crucify him ... it doesn't help, does it, to see the pictures of the house and the mortuary? I would have hated to see my house on television ... that's your own personal home ... what good will it do anybody to see that? It's almost that they want people to hurt.. the more they can hurt, the better it is!"

To these respondents, Scenario C was valid and acceptable, and even though some might be distressed by it and switch off, they knew that 'the public has a need to know', and indeed that some parents might want a greater exposure of their case than this scenario offered. The main concerns of these respondents were that relatives should know beforehand when the report was coming on and that sensational language should not be used.

> "It may be too impersonal for them, I think it's too impersonal ... If that's what the parents want, it's right, they're the most important ones to be considered ... There are some who want to shout, and others intensely private ... it's down to the families."

> "If sensitive wording is used, then OK. Sometimes it isn't ... words like 'slaughtered' are used, which is very distressing for families ... Not emotive or highly descriptive words, I don't think that's necessary."

> "Just because I sometimes get upset doesn't mean that these things don't happen ... I don't know how it would affect other victims' relatives but they would know that it had to be reported."

> "As long as they knew beforehand that it was going to be on ... you gear yourself up to it. You can get your body and brain ready to look at it – it's such a shock if they don't tell you."

Overall, these respondents found Scenario C the most suitable for early broadcast, with Scenario A for later, and in that they were in broad agreement with the other survivors, who tried to imagine what it must be like to be in their situation. Other survivors recognized that parents and relatives would feel 'awful', 'terrible', 'distressed' – but felt that probably no report would make them feel worse than they did already. Although there were some doubts about the necessity of including detail, and revulsion from that, overall, people felt that Scenario A was justified if it would help catch the murderer.

> "Almost anything is acceptable where the murder of children is involved."

> "A description of how the body was found would be very distressing for the person ... but then perhaps people need this level of detail to make them realize what could happen to their child ... it's in the interest of protecting other children ... I would know if it was my child anyway – I don't think I'd then mind other people knowing."

> "I have to say I find it distressing ... the reconstruction of anyone's life is bad. Describing description of bodies and search party is horrendous and awful."

> *"Bit gory – they're doing the same as Hillsborough."*
>
> *"I don't agree with this at all. There is no need for this at all."*
>
> *"I would switch it off because it's just reliving the agony and there but for the grace of God goes your own child."*
>
> *"I wouldn't – I'd feel for that person ... there should be interviews with relatives ... must let the media know what they're going through."*

Scenario B was generally condemned. It was 'tasteless', 'morbid' and would achieve nothing. Although a few did find it acceptable, most were critical.

> *"I think it's revelling in other people's misery ... I don't think there's a necessity to show you the bedroom of the victim."*
>
> *"That's sensationalism ... Not going to help anybody at all ... The mortuary – trying to include emotional feeling of friends and neighbours."*
>
> *"That's gory again. Not acceptable to the public. The mortuary ... no ... that's private ... what good is showing that?"*
>
> *"Too distressing ... makes me relive my own visit to the mortuary ... I couldn't even go to that part of the hospital now."*
>
> *"I wouldn't like to watch that. The mortuary affects me."*

In general, Scenario C was felt to be the least offensive although some felt it was too bland.

> *"I would watch it. It's news and I'd share the hurt with the parents."*
>
> *"It's ineffectual, lacks impact. People would hardly notice it – it's almost an everyday occurrence now."*

Overall, these respondents were divided between Scenarios A and C, with some preference for C because it would be least distressing to relatives of the murdered child. Interestingly, survivors of major disasters and traffic accidents were equally divided between these options, which makes them far more inclined to detailed coverage in this case than in their 'own' one of Hillsborough. The details are not, of course, really very comparable: in the Hillsborough case they were live, not reconstructed. Nevertheless, the point is perhaps worth noting.

Rape: three scenarios

Scenario A	Report of the crime showing a reconstruction of the events preceding the crime with a description by the victim in her own words.
Scenario B	Film of the scene of the crime, with a voice-over of events.
Scenario C	Factual statement by the news presenter, with only a picture of a map to show where it happened.

Three of those who had themselves been raped and some of the victims of assault thought it unlikely that a victim would want to participate in Scenario A.

> "If they managed to get a victim to describe it, I'd be very surprised ... I doubt if any rape victim is in her right mind at the time and that they would want to be reporting it."
>
> "A description by the victim in her own words – there's no way I'd have done that."
>
> "I don't think you'd get a genuine victim discussing it."
>
> "I'd just feel sorry for the victim, giving a description. How could anyone ask her, and how could she do it? ... It's totally unfair on the victim. She'd be too incoherent to give a good description anyway."
>
> "People don't realize at the time what it's actually going to do to their lives."
>
> "The victim would regret it afterwards."

Yet for others, this was acceptable, provided that the victim had given consent and provided that her identity was concealed.

> "It's not harming the girl that's been raped – giving the description in her own words. She would have wanted the man caught so would have agreed to the interview."

Overall, though, the survivors of rape, sexual abuse and assault rejected this scenario. People said they were 'disgusted' and 'sickened' by such reports; they thought the victim would feel 'anger' and 'horror' and that the relatives would feel 'very upset' or 'completely gutted'. As one victim of assault said:

> "I think anything like this is distressing to them. Before it didn't affect me really, but if anyone mentions rape now, that's it."

Scenario B was marginally better received by both the rape and the assault victims. Overall, interestingly, those whose own experiences came nearest to this hypothetical case – those who had been raped or suffered sexual abuse – were more accepting of it than the other assault victims. For one of these:

> "At least the victim and relatives who watched it would know something was being done and other people were being warned about what goes on."

But the majority of assault victims were very much opposed to this style of reporting and four felt such a report should not be shown at all.

> "I would switch it off because what can that possibly do for the victim? It would achieve nothing for the victim."
>
> "It would be hard enough for the victim to get over it without it being broadcast."

For assault victims, Scenario C was the most acceptable – although some felt that it gave too little detail and so would not have enough impact.

> "It's not much help to anyone who could have seen something because it doesn't give any details and most people wouldn't take much notice of it because it's just a report."
>
> "Bit weak ... as if it was nothing ... too subdued. If I was the parent I'd want the horror to come across."

Importantly, this was what the survivors of rape and sexual abuse tended to feel themselves. Three of the six felt that there was not enough detail for the report to be useful and one of those who did prefer this style nevertheless described it as 'gutless' and wondered whether it was realistic to expect television to make such a report.

Overall, the rape and sexual abuse victims were quite divided on what was the 'best' style of reporting. As one said:

> "You just have to take each incident, you can't really go on the whole, you have to take each incident as it happens."

And when it came to settling on one particular style, even the assault victims were not so much in favour of Scenario C as their previous comments might suggest: some went for the other two approaches. Overall, it was felt that reports should be factual and concentrate on the rapist – on the assumption that he was still at large. Finally, one survivor of rape pointed out that reporting should be balanced:

> "If you've shown at six different news times there's a rapist around, then they should repeat that they've caught him six times."

How did other survivors feel about the reporting of rape? Interestingly, this is the only topic which yields a clear divergence of views between people who had themselves been involved in the sort of event under discussion and those who had not. While those who had themselves suffered rape were *not* in favour of survivors giving their story immediately after the event, many of those who had been involved in murders and disasters or fatal traffic accidents saw nothing wrong in this – as long as the woman in question agreed. Some certainly had reservations. But many felt it would satisfy the public right – and need – to know, and maybe serve a wider social purpose too.

> "I don't like it. It's too sensational and only done to get a good story for TV ... When the victim had time to consider it afterwards, she might regret giving an interview like that ... If the police want witnesses they could appeal for help and just mention any relevant facts. No need to hear the girl's voice, especially if she sounded upset ... ."

> " ... it's too upsetting for the family of the victim to hear the details, and in her own voice ... A reconstruction could be shown with a reporter's voice giving the details and facts."

> "I don't think it should be shown, because it's invading the privacy of the victim – used as titillation."

> "Don't like it. Might suggest to someone else to do it."

> "I don't agree with it. The victim would be very upset to start with, and on telly would upset other people."

> "As she chooses to do so, it's OK. She maybe is trying to get her thing over ... how she feels and how hurt she is, to get justice."

> "I felt immense sympathy for her courage to relive ... it must have been very difficult and stressful."

> "The victim is involved and has chosen to do it, so the relatives would have to accept it because the choice is hers after all ... nothing would upset the victim as much as what has actually happened to her and she would want the person caught."

5 TOWARDS BOUNDARIES?

> "If more people talked about it and registered the fact they had been raped it might help ... I don't think the situation has improved that much."

> "Other victims would have to accept it as well. Life has to go on, it doesn't stop because of your own personal experiences."

Again, there was no strong opposition to Scenario B – and some people felt that it was preferable because it did not use the victim herself. Others, however, felt that weakened the report.

> "It's a better way of reporting, it doesn't actually use the victim."

> "It isn't as direct as listening to victim's voice."

> "It's more factual and didn't need to show the girl sobbing and being upset."

> "Not so severe ... from a family point of view. The voice-over – not so personal."

> "It wasn't distressing to me ... it's not really the scene of the crime. They just go down the same road that's all ... As long as it's not early on in the evening mainly because I then have to explain to my children what rape is."

> "I'd be interested to hear how they felt ... If you'd been a rape victim, you could perhaps give advice on how to avoid the situation possibly of being raped."

> " ... I think only if it's a child to report like this. An older person would benefit if they were involved."

Scenario C, these respondents felt, was unexceptionable, but of limited value.

> "It's news in a less emotional way and it could be of value in protecting other possible victims. It would alert people to the dangers in the area."

> "To save the relatives' feelings – instead of showing the actual place and hearing the victim's voice ... ."

> "No, that wouldn't have impact. If the police wanted assistance or witnesses, wouldn't have any effect."

> "It's too impersonal. Just a map doesn't really say anything."

> "Not really telling you much. People need to be hit hard to show and be aware what is happening."

Overall, these respondents opted for Scenario A as the most suitable way of reporting the rape – always provided that the victim herself was fully in agreement. The contrast with this and the feelings of those who had actually been raped is striking. Although all the respondents knew only too well from personal experience just how numbed and shocked people are after a traumatic event, it seems that not many of them thought of this when assessing Scenario A, concentrating instead on the vividness that personal statement brings to a report.

The contrast with sensitivity to survivors' feelings after Hillsborough is telling. Even other survivors did not seem to be able to understand just how intimate the experience of rape is to those who endure it.

Road traffic accident: three scenarios

Scenario A   Live report immediately after a motorway pile-up when the television crew arrives at the same time as the emergency vehicles.

Scenario B   Reports of events that happened earlier, with shots of the damaged vehicles, but no victims.

Scenario C   Factual report with a map showing drivers where the accident happened, with warnings to avoid the area.

Scenario A was the only 'live' report proposed apart from the one in Hillsborough, and most of those who had themselves been involved in fatal traffic accidents or major disasters were emphatically against it. They were concerned for the feelings of relatives as well as of victims, and made the practical point that television crews could impede the work of the rescue services.

> "This is out of order."

> "Very distasteful."

> "I just find it distasteful when they start filming ... victims ... it's not what I want to see on telly."

> "It's nasty."

> "Shocking."

> "Totally unacceptable."

> "Very distressing. Too shocking and only done for sensationalism."

> "Too distressing to watch ... nothing to be gained from showing it at this point except to score points over other channels."

> "I would switch off now ... because of my experiences and those people have families and the unbelievable agony is so unnecessary. I would have watched it before because it wouldn't have touched me personally."

> "People might see someone being cut out of a car ... might be the first knowledge that people have that relatives or friends were involved."

> "Some shots could prove so distressing that the relatives might not be able to get the scene out of their minds for a long time afterwards."

For those who had been involved in similar accidents, the reminders would be too painful:

> "It brings back all the trauma."

> "It would all come back – very distressing."

> "The families ... would feel terrible – an awful, painful reminder."

Yet for some respondents there could be a positive side to such live coverage.

> "People should see what happens and not be shielded, hoping it will make them think when doing stupid things on the road."

5 TOWARDS BOUNDARIES?

"It's not until people see how horrific they are – could make them think, and make it safer."

"There is a greater need for extra caution. Too many people think it couldn't happen to them."

"If it's showing the rescuers are doing a good job, it's good isn't it?"

Although a few people said they would switch it off, Scenario B was more generally acceptable to this group. Relatives would still be very distressed, but it was recognized that this would be so whatever the report.

"If you show past accidents, it always brings it back the same way."

"I don't think it's necessary to show damaged vehicles ... it leaves very little to the imagination."

"I have to find out these things. If you know about the things you can tell others and warn them."

"A mangled car is replaceable isn't it, but a person's not ... there's no victims involved in this bit here ... so it doesn't matter does it?"

"That's OK ... benefits to the motorist, think about speed, how they drive."

"People should be made aware of what can happen to them. Might make some people drive more carefully when they see the damaged vehicles."

For these respondents, Scenario C served an important practical purpose in that it warned other motorists to steer clear of the area and so most felt that it should be shown. For some, however, it was not detailed enough to have any impact.

"For the problem of reckless and dangerous driving, no."

Just over half the respondents in this group felt that Scenario B was the most suitable.

"It shows the accident without sensational ... shows the effect of the accident ... this should be brought home to motorists, they're lethal weapons."

"Might bring home to people the results ... getting the balance right between news and sensationalism."

A few, however, felt the shock value of Scenario A was necessary.

"It has the maximum impact ... and makes them think before they get into a motor vehicle again, and the way they handle that vehicle on the road."

"It covers the situation fully and points out the facts to other road users so they can see what can happen and perhaps they will take notice."

For most people among the survivors, however, Scenario A was the least suitable of all. Reactions were very similar to those on the Hillsborough coverage: reports should be vivid enough to shock people into an awareness of the magnitude of what had happened and into preventing recurrences, without inflicting avoidable distress on relatives and others who have survived a comparable disaster.

Reactions among the other survivor groups (not involved in fatal traffic accidents) were much the same as this:

> "Don't think it necessary to show smashed up bodies and blood. People are too complacent and need to be shocked into seeing what can happen, but not the actual victims ... ."

> "If it's live, some people could be seeing family or friends or their cars without any warning ... ."

> "Showing the results at the end, when the people have gone, that doesn't bother me. Showing a rescue going on, of dead and dying people is not acceptable. That's not entertainment or who does that help? That's a funny kind of definition of news. It's news, but it's news of other people's tragedies. That's going to be somebody's relative ... never mind the relative, the person themselves may have something to say about it, whether they want to be photographed in that position, or in that situation – if they survived."

By contrast, there was general support for Scenario B:

> "I feel it's in the public interest to be aware of the carnage that takes place on the road."

> "It's not as upsetting to the victim's family and shots of the damaged vehicles might remind people to be more careful."

> "News is a necessary evil. We have to know what has happened and what can happen. Sometimes it can serve as a warning to reckless drivers."

> "It does us all good to show us if we don't drive carefully what can happen to us. It's all news ... as long as it's not personal. If you saw one of your family's cars involved, it would be too dreadful, should be left until relatives are informed."

For this group, as the other, Scenario C was acceptable as factual information, although too bland to carry much weight beyond warning people to avoid the area. There was some little support for Scenario A.

> "When a tragedy has happened you can't change it ... the truth has to come out eventually."

> "If it was my family, A. I could see what was going on. If it didn't involve them, if it was just news, then B."

But overall, live coverage of the motorway pile-up was vehemently rejected.

> "Because it's voyeurism to a certain extent ... it's wrong for people to find out about accidents to friends and relatives from TV."

> "It just shocks ... just for good TV. No thought to the relatives who might get a terrible shock ... shouldn't be shown live."

5 TOWARDS BOUNDARIES?

In general

What general points about reporting styles can be drawn from survivors' responses? Three main criteria for acceptability to them seem to stand out. Reports should cause *minimal distress* to survivors, relatives and other people who have suffered these tragedies. They should be *useful*. And those most involved should exercise the greatest possible *control* over what is reported.

Throughout the discussions, these survivors were consistently trying to balance humanitarian concerns with their recognition that they, and others in similar situations, were inevitably involved in events which were newsworthy and of interest to the viewing public. Importantly, though, it was only in the case of live coverage (discussed below) that their concern to protect people from distress overrode all other considerations. These survivors were striving for balance between personal and public interests – and recognized that often these in fact coincided.

Distress was only justified, however, if the report could demonstrate its *usefulness*. Television and radio reports could be useful in helping to catch murderers or rapists. They could usefully warn viewers to make sure that they and their children avoided certain areas, or they could serve as a more general grim reminder that there are some extremely dangerous people about. They could, on an immediately practical level, warn drivers to avoid the sites of pile-ups, and more generally, they could serve as a reminder of the consequences of dangerous and foolish driving. They could – and should? – expose the human frailties and negligences that had contributed to major disasters and so help to minimize the danger of such disasters happening again.

When reports seemed to do none of these things, then these survivors condemned them. They saw no point – and nothing but pain for relatives and other survivors – in television shots of mortuaries and the houses where dead children had lived. They saw no point – and even danger – in coverage that could identify where the victims of violence lived. And they condemned live coverage of disasters and motorway pile-ups because this would not only cause huge distress to families, but achieve nothing beyond what edited accounts and interviews could do.

This last is probably the most contentious reaction of all and broadcasters might feel its possible consequences are unacceptable, given their duty to inform. The public might also find it difficult to accept. Two thirds of the respondents in the large survey, after all, thought the reporting of the Hillsborough disaster had been 'well-handled'. The extremely strong reactions against the live coverage – not just from survivors of that and comparable disasters, but from the survivor sample as a whole – say something different. What these survivors were effectively after was a ban on live coverage, and even on edited coverage until after the relatives had been informed; some would have made even that conditional on relatives giving their permission.

So what sorts of *control* were these survivors talking about? The word came up fairly frequently in the interviews, though not attached to discussion of how the sort of media discretion they wanted might be enforced. Yet the issue of 'ownership' of the events into which they had been catapulted was clearly of tremendous importance for these survivors. Their own accounts of their experiences of the media underlined time and again just how much they felt that control over *their* tragedy has been usurped. The general acceptance of scenarios that included or focused on interviews with survivors, the insistence on their consent to these, is maybe one way of reasserting people's control over their own story at a time when it can so often seem dangerously lost or painfully usurped in the rush of public interest. At another level, survivors often spoke of the need for warning before potentially painful items were screened, so that at least they had more control over whether they watched them. (Some, of course, would prefer that some items simply were not screened at all.)

In the end, perhaps, what these survivors were talking about is directly related to two of the foremost needs of people who have suffered sudden and violent bereavement. They want television coverage to help people in such a situation to find some meaning in their personal tragedy (at least it may help to prevent future ones). And they want it to enable those who have been thrown into helplessness by the sudden wrenching of their world from its accustomed patterns to recover at least some measure of control over the events in which they are so painfully and intimately involved.

APPENDIX 1: THE SURVEYS

General survey

The Harris Research Centre was commissioned by the Broadcasting Standards Council to conduct a quantitative study about attitudes to the broadcasting of acts of terrorism, natural disasters, and other national disasters. The study (conducted in March 1990) also investigated attitudes to the treatment of victims by the media. The Harris Research Centre recruited a nationally representative sample of 1050 adults.

Within the main sample the survey found a sub-sample of 188 respondents who had been, or were related to, survivors of natural disasters, accidents or crimes.

Survivors' survey

In June 1990, the Broadcasting Standards Council asked the British Market Research Bureau (BMRB) to investigate the views of survivors of violent crimes, accidents and disasters, and those of close relatives of victims.

There were considerable difficulties in recruiting respondents for the Survey but, in the end, BMRB contacted a total of 52 people through a number of support schemes and self-help groups, including Victim Support. Two further people who had been involved in the Hillsborough stadium disaster contacted BMRB directly after they heard of the study on BBC Radio Merseyside.

BMRB conducted 6 pilot depth interviews, each tape-recorded and lasting two hours or more. From these, it developed:

– a depth interview guide for further interviews by its executives.

– a semi-structured interview for trained interviewers to use.

All the interviews were completed between 1 November 1990 and 26 February 1991, and ranged around the country according to availability of contacts.

	Total	Pilot interviews	Depth interviews	Semi-structured interviews
Murder/manslaughter	19	3	5	11
Rape/sexual abuse/assault	19	0	6	13
Disaster/major accidents	16	1	1	14
TOTAL	54	4	12	38

Murder and manslaughter

There were 19 respondents in this category, contacted through local Victim Support groups and/or Parents of Murdered Children, all but one of the mothers of (mostly adult) victims; one father also joined the interview with his wife. The interviews were either in the respondents' own homes or, usually in privacy, at the homes of counsellors.

Some facts about the deaths:

–9 sons, 9 daughters, 1 other relative;

–6 in the street, 6 in victims/culprit's home, 7 elsewhere, sometimes the survey respondent was present;

–7 resulting from a dispute with individuals unconnected with the victim, 7 where the culprit was emotionally linked with the victim, 5 other cases or unknown;

–8 by stabbing/battery, 5 by strangling/battery, 2 by battery alone, 4 by other causes;

–4 abroad, 15 in Great Britain;

–16 with culprit found guilty, 3 with unknown culprit.

Rape, sexual abuse and assault

Of the 6 depth interviews:

–3 were with rape victims;

–1 was with the mother of a young girl who was raped;

–1 was with the (now adult) victim of childhood sexual abuse;

–1 was with the mother of a child who had been sexually abused.

The 13 semi-structured interviews were with people who had been physically assaulted.

In two of the rape and one of the sexual abuse cases, there had been a court hearing.

Two victims were raped in their own homes by intruders. The events took place several years before the interviews.

All but a few of the assault cases had come to court, with charges ranging from attempted murder to wounding with intent. All the assaults had taken place within the two years before the interviews.

Disasters and road traffic accidents

The 16 respondents in this group had been involved in a variety of incidents:

–4 had been involved in, or had relatives involved in, fatal car accidents;

–11 had been involved in, or had relatives involved in, major disasters.

One in-depth interview was taken from each group and the remainder were semi-structured. The disasters included Hillsborough, the Marchioness, the M1 air crash and the Zeebrugge ferry. In each case a friend or relative had died in the disaster; sometimes the respondent had survived the same disaster.

This project was led by Simon Orton, Director in charge of BMRB's Survey Research Division. He has worked at BMRB for over 18 years, since graduating from Oxford.

The project was controlled by Sue Brooker (Associate Director) who has worked at BMRB for seven years, supported by Helen Pillenger (Senior Research Executive) who has 3 years experience of survey research at BMRB.

These three executives, supported by Susannah Quick (Associate Director), conducted the Depth Interviews and designed the Semi-Structured interview.

APPENDIX 2: VIEWING BEHAVIOUR

Respondents to the survivors' study considered the following:

Television Series	Films
Ruth Rendell Mysteries	The Krays
London's Burning	Lethal Weapon
Inspector Morse	Sudden Impact
Miami Vice	Beverly Hills Cop 2
Crimewatch UK	Mad Max
Blackeyes	The Witches of Eastwick
The Bill	Friday 13th
Bergerac	Psycho III
The Sweeny	Fatal Attraction
EastEnders	Privates on Parade
Brookside	Personal Services
	Aliens 2
	Nine and a Half Weeks
	The Towering Inferno
	Ghostbusters II

APPENDIX 3: ACCEPTABILITY OF TELEVISION REPORTS

The survivors' sample considered the following television items for acceptability:

1. The scene of a major incident after bodies have been removed.
2. The funeral of someone who has been the victim of a terrorist attack.
3. Close-up shots of blood-streaked pavements where victims fell.
4. The scene of a major incident taken from a distance so that the dead or injured are not recognisable.
5. The scene of a major incident showing dead or seriously injured people who are recognisable.
6. Interviews with bereaved relatives after the death of a member of their family.
7. Pictures of people who have been bereaved and are in a very emotional state.
8. Interviews in hospital with people who have been the victim of violent crime.
9. Interviews with people in hospital suffering from a terminal illness.
10. Pictures of victims being visited in hospital by members of the Government or Royal Family.

The large-scale sample considered all but item 3 for acceptability and for showing before and after the Watershed. It also considered 3 further items:

1. Dramatic reconstruction of natural disasters with actors as victims.
2. Funeral of a victim of a natural disaster.
3. Interview in hospital with victims of natural disaster.

Both the survivor and large-scale samples considered further items for acceptability and timing of transmission:

1. Reconstruction of last sightings of murder victims or missing persons (survivors).
2. Reconstructions of violent crime with actors (large-scale survey).

In addition, the survivors' sample considered whether the following should be broadcast before or after the Watershed and in what degree of detail:

1. Civil disturbances like Brixton, Toxteth.
2. Destruction caused by terrorist bombs.
3. Scenes from major football incidents such as Hillsborough.
4. Major fires such as King's Cross.
5. Scenes from major transport disasters such as aeroplane or train crashes.
6. Crowd disorder around sports grounds.

APPENDIX 4: THE AUTHOR

After leaving Cambridge University, where she read history, **Ann Shearer** spent six years at the *Guardian*, first as a reporter and then as social services correspondent. Since then, she has worked freelance, with spells as a *Guardian* leader writer and Society Tomorrow page editor. During the 1970s and early '80s, she worked with Campaign for Mentally Handicapped People, of which she was co-founder, and with the international network of l'Arche communities. Lecturing and consultancy took her around Britain and to North America, Asia, Australia and New Zealand. Her books include *Disability: Whose Handicap?* (1981), *Building Community* (1986) and *Woman: Her Changing Image* (1987).

OTHER CONTRIBUTORS

Dr David Docherty, previously Research Director at the Broadcasting Standards Council, is currently Head of Information Services, Broadcasting Research Department, BBC.

Katherine Lannon is Press and Programmes Officer at the Broadcasting Standards Council

Andrea Millwood Hargrave, previously Director of Planning (Marketing) at British Satellite Broadcasting, is Research Director at the Broadcasting Standards Council.

BSC PUBLICATIONS

A Code of Practice
November 1989
This publication is available free of charge from the Council

Broadcasting Standards Council Annual Report 1988-89 and *Code of Practice*

Broadcasting Standards Council Annual Report 1989-90 and 1990-1991
Available from the Council £4.00

BSC Monograph Series

A Measure of Uncertainty – The Effects of the Mass Media
by Dr Guy Cumberbatch and Dr Dennis Howitt
Co-publishers John Libbey and Co Ltd, 1989, £18.00

Survivors and the Media
by Ann Shearer
Co-publishers John Libbey and Co Ltd, 1991, £7.50

BSC Annual Review

Public Opinion and Broadcasting Standards – 1
Violence in Television Fiction
by Dr David Docherty
Co-publishers John Libbey and Co Ltd, 1990, £7.50

Public Opinion and Broadcasting Standards – 2
Taste and Decency in Broadcasting
by Andrea Millwood Hargrave
Co-publishers John Libbey and Co Ltd, 1991, £7.50

BSC Research Working Papers 1990

I. *Children, Television and Morality*,
Dr Anne Sheppard, University of Leeds;

II. *Television and Fantasy: An Exploratory Study*,
The Communications Research Group, Aston University

III. *Morality, Television and the Pre-adolescent,*
Research International, Young Minds

IV. *Television Advertising and Sex Role Stereotyping,*
The Communications Research Group, Aston University
Working papers available from the BSC, £3.00 per copy.

Leaflets

Making Complaints
Available from the BSC free of charge

Future Publications

Television and the Public Interest
The Protection of Vulnerable Values in European Television
Edited by Professor Jay G Blumler

Women Viewing Violence: How Women Interpret Violence on Television
University of Stirling, Film and Media Research Institute
and Institute for the Study of Violence

Study into Attitudes towards the use of Bad Language in Broadcasting
Edited by Andrea Millwood Hargrave

THE BROADCASTING STANDARDS COUNCIL

The Broadcasting Standards Council's remit concerns the portrayal in television and radio programmes and broadcast advertisements of violence, sexual conduct and matters of taste and decency.

The Council was first established on a pre-statutory basis by the Government in May 1988. It became a statutory body under the Broadcasting Act 1990, with effect from 1 January 1991.

The Council has five main tasks:

1. To draw up and from time to time review a Code of Practice in consultation with the broadcasting authorities and others. The Broadcasting Act places a duty on the broadcasters to reflect the BSC's Code in their own codes and programme guidelines. The BSC's Code was published in November 1989 and circulated widely among broadcasters, interested organisations and members of the public.

2. To monitor programmes and to make reports on the areas within the Council's remit.

3. To commission research into such matters as the nature and effects on attitudes and behaviour of the portrayal of violence and of sex in programmes and advertisements and standards of taste and decency.

4. To consider and make findings on complaints.

5. To represent the UK on international bodies concerned with setting standards for television programmes.

Broadcasting Standards Council
5-8 The Sanctuary
London SW1P 3JS

Tel: 071-233 0544
Fax: 071-233 0397

Media titles available from John Libbey

ACAMEDIA RESEARCH MONOGRAPHS

Satellite Television in Western Europe
Richard Collins
Hardback ISBN 0 86196 203 6

Beyond the Berne Convention
Copyright, Broadcasting and the Single European Market
Vincent Porter
Hardback ISBN 0 86196 267 2

The Media Dilemma: Freedom and Choice or Concentrated Power?
Gareth Locksley
Hardback ISBN 0 86196 230 3

Nuclear Reactions: A Study in Public Issue Television
John Corner, Kay Richardson and Natalie Fenton
Hardback ISBN 0 86196 251 6

Transnationalization of Television in Western Europe
Preben Sepstrup
Hardback ISBN 0 86196 280 X

The People's Voice: Local Television and Radio in Europe
Nick Jankowski, Ole Prehn and James Stappers
Hardback ISBN 0 86196 322 9

BBC ANNUAL REVIEWS

Annual Review of BBC Broadcasting Research: No XV - 1989
Peter Menneer (ed)
Paperback ISBN 0 86196 209 5

Annual Review of BBC Broadcasting Research: No XVI - 1990
Peter Menneer (ed)
Paperback ISBN 0 86196 265 6

Published in association with UNESCO

Video World-Wide: An International Study
Manuel Alvarado (ed)
Paperback ISBN 0 86196 143 9

Media titles available from John Libbey

BROADCASTING STANDARDS COUNCIL PUBLICATIONS

A Measure of Uncertainty: The Effects of the Mass Media
Guy Cumberbatch and Dennis Howitt
Foreword by Lord Rees-Mogg
Hardback ISBN 0 86196 231 1

Violence in Television Fiction: Public Opinion and Broadcasting Standards
David Docherty
Paperback ISBN 0 86196 284 2

Survivors and the Media
Ann Shearer
Paperback ISBN 0 86196 332 6

Taste and Decency in Broadcasting
Andrea Millwood Hargrave
Paperback ISBN 0 86196 331 8

BROADCASTING RESEARCH UNIT MONOGRAPHS

Quality in Television – Programmes, Programme-makers, Systems
Richard Hoggart (ed)
Paperback ISBN 0 86196 237 0

Keeping Faith? Channel Four and its Audience
David Docherty, David E. Morrison and Michael Tracey
Paperback ISBN 0 86196 158 7

Invisible Citizens: British Public Opinion and the Future of Broadcasting
David E. Morrison
Paperback ISBN 0 86196 111 0

School Television in Use
Diana Moses and Paul Croll
Paperback ISBN 0 86196 308 3

Media titles available from John Libbey

**Published in association with
THE ARTS COUNCIL of GREAT BRITAIN**

Picture This: Media Representations of Visual Art and Artists
Philip Hayward (ed)
Paperback ISBN 0 86196 126 9

Culture, Technology and Creativity
Philip Hayward (ed)
Paperback ISBN 0 86196 266 4

ITC TELEVISION RESEARCH MONOGRAPHS

Television in Schools
Robin Moss, Christopher Jones and Barrie Gunter
Hardback ISBN 0 86196 314 8

IBA TELEVISION RESEARCH MONOGRAPHS

**Teachers and Television:
A History of the IBA's Educational Fellowship Scheme**
Josephine Langham
Hardback ISBN 0 86196 264 8

Godwatching: Viewers, Religion and Television
Michael Svennevig, Ian Haldane, Sharon Spiers and Barrie Gunter
Hardback ISBN 0 86196 198 6 Paperback ISBN 0 86196 199 4

Violence on Television: What the Viewers Think
Barrie Gunter and Mallory Wober
Hardback ISBN 0 86196 171 4 Paperback ISBN 0 86196 172 2

Home Video and the Changing Nature of Television Audience
Mark Levy and Barrie Gunter
Hardback ISBN 0 86196 175 7 Paperback ISBN 0 86196 188 9

Patterns of Teletext Use in the UK
Bradley S. Greenberg and Carolyn A. Lin
Hardback ISBN 0 86196 174 9 Paperback ISBN 0 86196 187 0

Attitudes to Broadcasting Over the Years
Barrie Gunter and Michael Svennevig
Hardback ISBN 0 86196 173 0 Paperback ISBN 0 86196 184 6

Media titles available from John Libbey

Television and Sex Role Stereotyping
Barrie Gunter
Hardback ISBN 0 86196 095 5 Paperback ISBN 0 86196 098 X

Television and the Fear of Crime
Barrie Gunter
Hardback ISBN 0 86196 118 8 Paperback ISBN 0 86196 119 6

Behind and in Front of the Screen - Television's Involvement with Family Life
Barrie Gunter and Michael Svennevig
Hardback ISBN 0 86196 123 4 Paperback ISBN 0 86196 124 2

UNIVERSITY OF MANCHESTER BROADCASTING SYMPOSIUM

And Now for the BBC
Proceedings of the 22nd Symposium 1991
Nod Miller and Rod Allen (eds)
Paperback ISBN 0 86196 318 0

Poynter Institute
92009836

```
PN          Shearer, Ann, 1943-
1992.6      Survivors and the
.S541       media
1991
```

DATE DUE